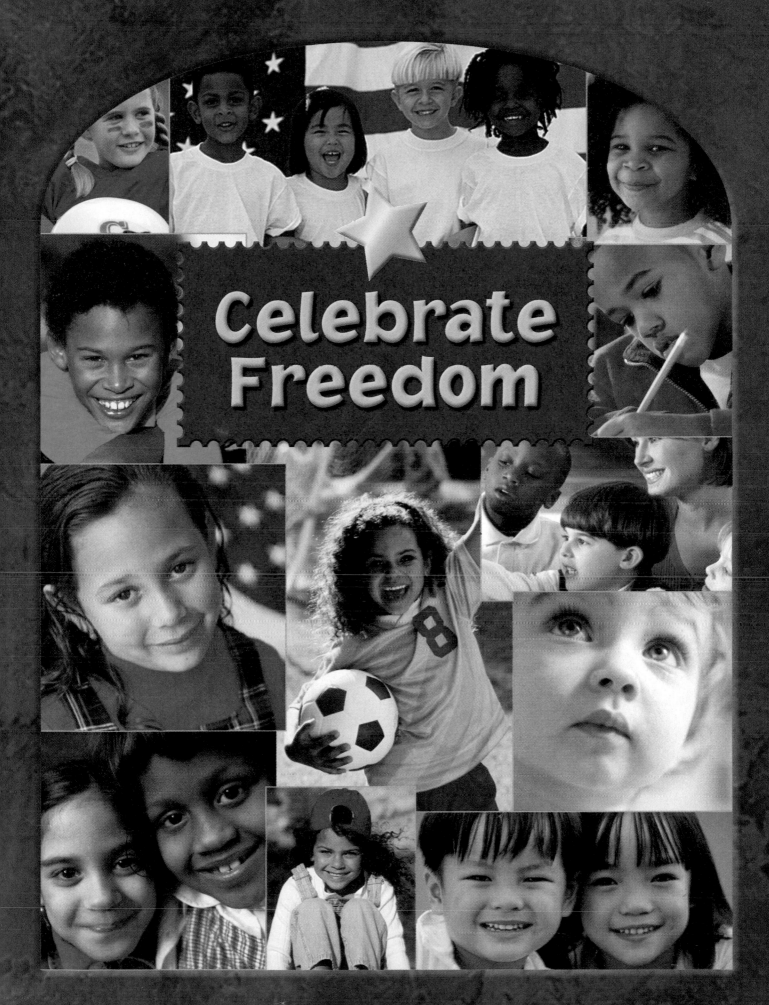

Celebrate Freedom

Celebrate Freedom

Our country has three important documents. These are the Declaration of Independence, the Constitution, and the Bill of Rights. Read here to find out what these documents say.

Declaration of Independence, 1776

We want to be free from England. The king of England does not treat us fairly. Everyone has the right to life, freedom, and to find happiness. We believe that everyone is created equal.

- **Why did Americans want to be free from England?**

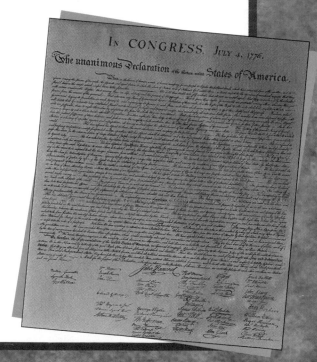

Constitution of the United States of America, 1789

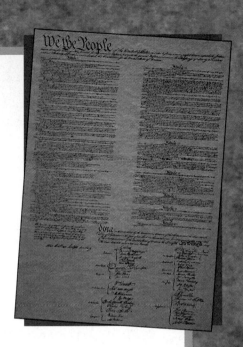

We, the people, want to make a better country. Each state will help to decide on our laws. We will make laws that treat everyone fairly. We will choose our own leaders.

- **Who will choose our leaders?**

Bill of Rights, 1791

We are now adding ten more rights to our Constitution. We all want to have the same freedoms. These include:

- freedom to pray as we choose
- freedom to say what we think
- freedom to write what we think
- **What does the Bill of Rights say?**

Celebrate Freedom

Materials:
- Construction paper
- Old magazines
- Scissors
- Glue
- Stapler
- Pencil or marker

Make a Freedom Book

Choose pictures that show freedom.

1. On one sheet, write the word *Freedom*. This will be the book cover.

2. Cut out pictures showing freedom from old magazines. Choose pictures that mean freedom to you.

3. Glue the pictures onto the sheets of construction paper.

4. Staple the pages together to make a book.

Make a Freedom Word Web

Materials:
• Paper
• Pencil
• Markers

1 Make a list of words that mean freedom to you.

2 Draw a word web. Write the word *Freedom* in the center.

3 Fill in the word web with your other freedom words.

Celebrate Freedom

The Pledge of Allegiance

I pledge allegiance to the Flag of the United States of America and to the Republic for which it stands, one Nation under God, indivisible, with liberty and justice for all.

The National Anthem

Oh, say, can you see, by the dawn's early light,
What so proudly we hailed at the twilight's last gleaming?
Whose broad stripes and bright stars, thro' the perilous fight,
O'er the ramparts we watched, were so gallantly streaming.
And the rockets' red glare, the bombs bursting in air,
Gave proof through the night that our flag was still there.
Oh, say, does that star-spangled banner yet wave
O'er the land of the free and the home of the brave?

A7

Americans Speak About Freedom

Our country promises freedom to everyone. Our leaders ask us to keep that promise.

Abraham Lincoln

16th President of the United States

"This nation . . . shall have a new birth of freedom, and government of the people, by the people, for the people shall [never end]."

Barbara Jordan

Congresswoman from Texas

"What the people want is very simple. They want an America as good as its promise."

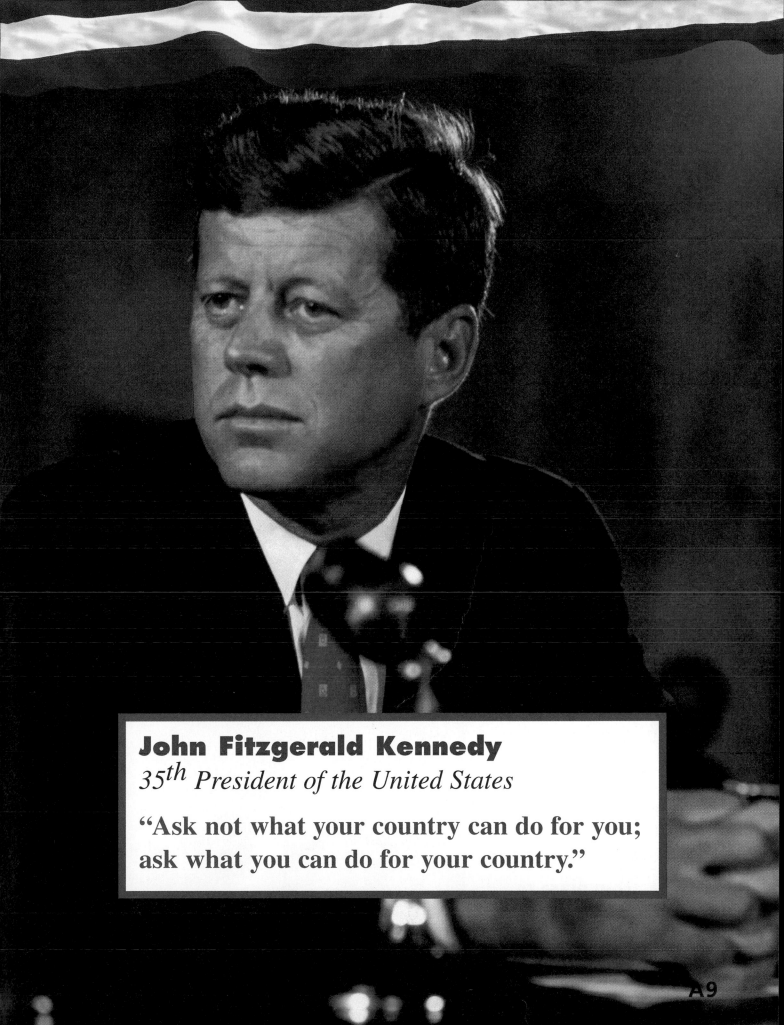

John Fitzgerald Kennedy
35th President of the United States

"Ask not what your country can do for you; ask what you can do for your country."

Geography

RUSSIA

Alaska

CANADA

Bering Sea

Gulf of Alaska

PACIFIC OCEAN

Washington

Columbia River

Missouri River

Montana

Oregon

Idaho

Wyoming

PACIFIC OCEAN

Nevada

Great Salt Lake

Utah

Colorado

Arkansas

California

Colorado River

Kauai

Hawaii

Nihau

Molokai

Oahu

Maui

Arizona

New Mexico

Hawaii

MEX

Americans on the Move

The United States is a big country. Americans need roads, canals, and railroads to get around. What is your favorite way to travel?

 What is one way Americans move from place to place?

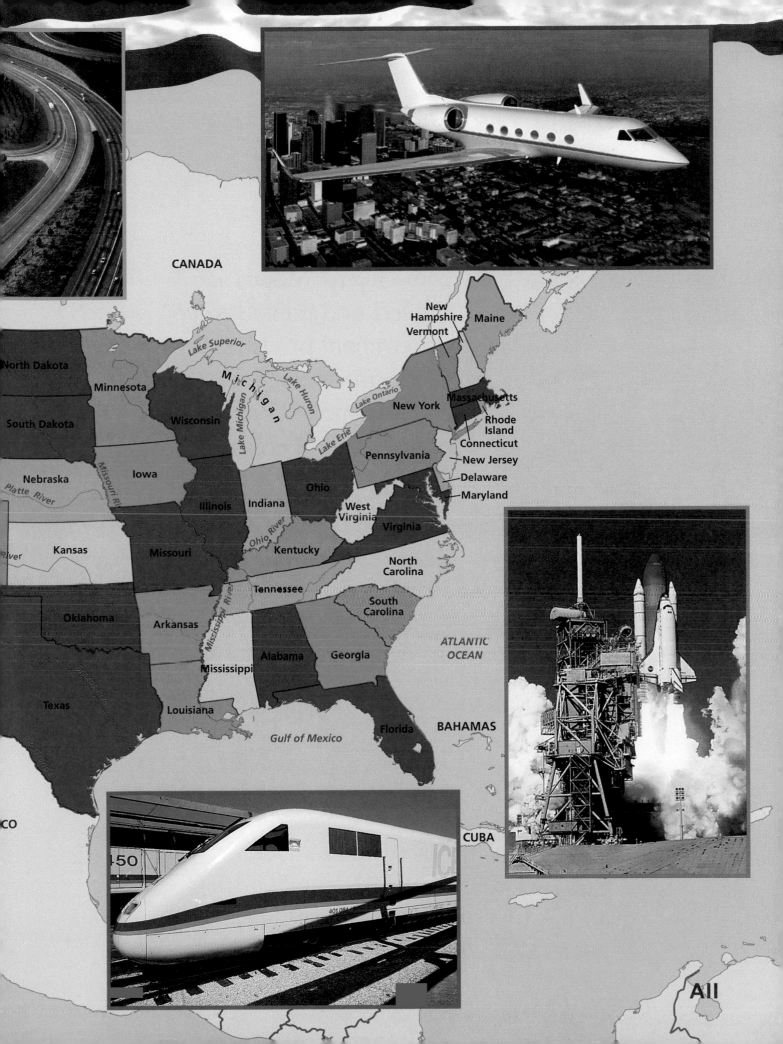

CANADA

North Dakota

Minnesota

South Dakota

Lake Superior

Michigan

Lake Huron

Lake Michigan

Lake Ontario

Lake Erie

New Hampshire

Vermont

Maine

Wisconsin

Nebraska

Iowa

Missouri River

Platte River

Kansas

River

Illinois

Indiana

Ohio

Ohio River

New York

Massachusetts

Rhode Island

Connecticut

New Jersey

Delaware

Maryland

Pennsylvania

West Virginia

Virginia

Missouri

Kentucky

North Carolina

Oklahoma

Arkansas

Tennessee

Mississippi River

South Carolina

Texas

Mississippi

Alabama

Georgia

Louisiana

ATLANTIC OCEAN

Gulf of Mexico

Florida

BAHAMAS

CUBA

CO

450

ICE

401 054

AII

Economics

Making Money

Where does money come from? Money is printed and minted. Our government prints paper money. Our government also stamps metal to make coins. This is called minting coins.

✓ **Who makes our money?**

Government

Making Laws that Are Fair

Laws are rules for a community, state, or country. People in our government make laws. They try to make laws that are fair. Many Americans have worked to make sure our laws are fair to everyone.

What are laws?

Martin Luther King, Jr. worked to make sure our laws treat all Americans the same.

Susan B. Anthony worked to make sure women were allowed to vote.

Citizenship

Community Heroes

Heroes are people who help others. Your town has heroes who work to protect everyone in the community. Firefighters put out dangerous fires. Police officers make sure your community is safe.

What do police officers do?

A14

Culture

American Arts and Crafts

America has many cultures. *Culture* means the special ways people do things. Making arts and crafts is one part of culture. Artists often use things from nearby to make artwork.

 What is one part of culture?

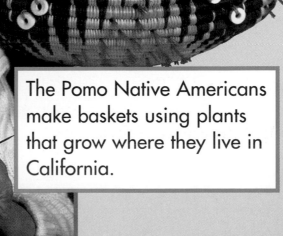

Some people who live in the mountains of North Carolina carve oak wood. Others make dolls from cornhusks.

The Pomo Native Americans make baskets using plants that grow where they live in California.

Science, Technology, and Society

1900

1922

1955

2000

100 Years of Cars

In the United States, cars are probably our most important way to travel. One hundred years ago, few people had cars. Early cars had small engines. They were no faster than a horse and buggy. Today, cars can travel great distances in a short time.

 What is one way that cars have changed over time?

Macmillan/McGraw-Hill

We Live Together

National Geographic

Mc Graw Hill

About the Cover: A United States flag made by a child appears in front of a view of the village green in Lyndonville, Vermont.

A18

Macmillan/McGraw-Hill

We Live Together

James A. Banks

Richard G. Boehm

Kevin P. Colleary

Gloria Contreras

A. Lin Goodwin

Mary A. McFarland

Walter C. Parker

NATIONAL
GEOGRAPHIC

**Mc Graw Hill Macmillan
McGraw-Hill**

New York

PROGRAM AUTHORS

Dr. James A. Banks
Russell F. Stark University Professor and Director of the Center for Multicultural Education
University of Washington
Seattle, Washington

Dr. Richard G. Boehm
Jesse H. Jones Distinguished Chair in Geographic Education and Director, The Gilbert M. Grosvenor Center for Geographic Education
Southwest Texas State University
San Marcos, Texas

Dr. Kevin P. Colleary
Curriculum and Teaching Department
Hunter College
City University of New York
New York, New York

Dr. Gloria Contreras
Professor of Education
University of North Texas
Denton, Texas

Dr. A. Lin Goodwin
Associate Professor of Education
Department of Curriculum and Teaching
Teachers College
Columbia University
New York, New York

Dr. Mary A. McFarland
Social Studies Education Consultant, K-12
St. Louis, Missouri

Dr. Walter C. Parker
Professor of Education and Chair of Social Studies Education
University of Washington
Seattle, Washington

NATIONAL GEOGRAPHIC
Washington, D.C.

HISTORIANS/SCHOLARS

Dr. Joyce Appleby
Professor of History
University of California, Los Angeles
Los Angeles, California

Dr. Alan Brinkley
Professor of American History
Columbia University
New York, New York

Dr. Nancy Cott
Stanley Woodward Professor of History and American Studies
Yale University
New Haven, Connecticut

Dr. James McPherson
George Henry Davis Professor of American History
Princeton University
Princeton, New Jersey

Dr. Donald A. Ritchie
Associate Historian of the United States Senate Historical Office
Washington, D.C.

PROGRAM CONSULTANTS

Betty Ruth Baker, M.Ed
Assistant Professor of Curriculum and Instruction
Early Childhood Specialist
School of Education
Baylor University
Waco, Texas

Dr. Randolph B. Campbell
Regents' Professor of History
University of North Texas
Denton, Texas

Dr. Steven Cobb
Director, Center for Economic Education
Chair, Department of Economics
University of North Texas
Denton, Texas

Frank de Varona, Ed.S.
Visiting Associate Professor
Florida International University
Miami, Florida

Dr. John L. Esposito
Professor of Religion and International Affairs, and Director of the Center for Christian-Muslim Understanding
Georgetown University
Washington, D.C.

READING INSTRUCTION CONSULTANTS

M. Frankie Dungan, M.Ed.
Reading/Language Arts Consultant, K–6
Mansfield, Texas

Antonio A. Fierro
Program Director for the Texas Reading Initiative, Region 19
El Paso, Texas

Carol Ritchey, M.Ed.
Reading Specialist
Tarver Rendon Elementary School
Burleson, Texas

Dr. William H. Rupley
Professor of Reading Education
Distinguished Research Fellow
Department of Teaching, Learning and Culture
College of Education
Texas A&M University
College Station, Texas

GRADE LEVEL CONSULTANTS

Calvin Baxter
Director of Humanities
Buffalo Board of Education
Buffalo, New York

Patty Evans
Field Coordinator of Social Studies
Syracuse City School District
Syracuse, New York

Gloria Garnes
Second Grade Teacher
Arnold Elementary School
San Antonio, Texas

Barbara Harrison
Second Grade Teacher
Martin Weiss Elementary School
Dallas, Texas

Betty Johnson
Past President
Dade County Council for the Social Studies
Homestead, Florida

Tammy Lanterman
Second Grade Teacher
Holland Elementary School
Satellite Beach, Florida

Judith Runnels
Second Grade Teacher
Eugene Field Elementary School
Beaumont, Texas

Joanne Sadler
Supervisor of Curriculum
Buffalo Board of Education
Buffalo, New York

Susan Temple
Social Studies Consultant
North Carolina Public Schools
Zebulon, North Carolina

CONTRIBUTING WRITERS

Dinah Zike
Comfort, Texas

Kathy Fitzgibbon
Austin, Texas

Karen Lowther
Austin, Texas

Linda Scher
Raleigh, North Carolina

Wendy Vierow
New Paltz, New York

RFB&D 🎧
learning through listening

Students with print disabilities may be eligible to obtain an accessible, audio version of the pupil edition of this textbook. Please call Recording for the Blind & Dyslexic at 1-800-221-4792 for complete information.

Acknowledgments

The publisher gratefully acknowledges permission to reprint the following copyrighted material:

"Until We Built a Cabin" from **Always Wondering** by Aileen Fisher. Copyright ©1991 by Aileen Fisher. HarperCollins Publishers. All rights reserved.

From "Washington's Farewell to His Officers" from **Memoir of Colonel Benjamin Tallmadge**. Copyright ©1968 Arno Press, Inc. The New York Times & Arno Press, NY. Used by permission. From "Slavery, Constitution and War (Letter to A. G. Hodges)" from **Abraham Lincoln: Speeches and Writings, 1859–1865**. New York: The Library of America. Copyright ©1989 The Claremont Institute. October 24, 2001. www.leaderu.com/humanities/lIncolnspeech.html. Used by permission.

From **Immigrants** by Martin W. Sandler. Copyright ©1995 by Eagle Productions, Inc. HarperCollins Publishers. Used by permission.

(continued on page R22)

Macmillan/McGraw-Hill

A Division of The **McGraw·Hill** *Companies*

Printed in the United States of America

ISBN 0-02-149263-8

5 6 7 8 9 027/043 06 05 04 03

Contents

REFERENCE SECTION

FEATURES

CHARTS AND GRAPHS

MAPS

The Eight Strands of Social Studies

There are many parts to social studies.
Look at the pictures to learn more.

History

- The story of the past

Economics

- Meeting our needs and wants

Geography

- People and places on Earth

Government

- Leaders and laws

Citizenship

- Rules and responsibilities

Culture

- The way of life shared by a group of people

Science, Technology, and Society

- New ideas and tools changing the way people live

Social Studies Skills

- Reading, thinking, and studying

Thinking About Reading

Thinking about what you read helps you learn the information better. Use the four tips below to become a good social studies reader.

1. **Preview the lesson.** Preview means to look something over before you start. Read the title. Look at the pictures and maps.

2. **Ask yourself questions** before you read. You might ask, "What will I learn in this lesson?"

3. **Read and reread.** Read the sentences carefully. Look up the meanings of words you don't know. Then reread the sentences.

4. **Review, or think about**, what you have read. Did you find the answers to your questions?

1 **Preview.**
The title and pictures tell me this lesson will be about flags of other countries.

2 **Ask.**
I ask myself, "What will I learn about flags?"

3 **Read.**
I read each sentence. I need to look up the word **symbol**. Then I will reread the sentence with the word **symbol**.

4 **Review.**
I think about what I learned about flags.

Flags of Many Countries

Every country has a flag. Each flag is a symbol for that country. Flags sometimes show something about that country.

Canada's flag has a maple leaf in the middle. Many maple trees grow in Canada. The maple leaf shows something about the country of Canada.

Mexico's flag has an eagle in the middle. The eagle is an important Mexican symbol.

Mexico's flag

Canada's flag

H4

Using Pictures

You can learn more about what you read by looking carefully at the pictures.

How to Use Pictures

First, look at the picture. Then, ask yourself:

- What does the picture show?

- Does the picture have a label? What does the label say?

Look at the chart below. It tells you two things that you learned from looking at the picture.

Peninsula

Peninsula

| The picture shows land and water. | The land has water on all sides but one. |

Look carefully at the picture below. Then copy the chart that is under the picture. Fill in the chart to tell two things that the picture shows.

Island

```
        Island
       /      \
  ┌────────┐  ┌────────┐
  │        │  │        │
  └────────┘  └────────┘
```

Practice Activity!

Look at pages 80–81. What do the pictures show? Explain how you know what they are.

WELCOME TO Washington, D.C.

Winter in Washington, D.C. can be cold, wet, and sometimes snowy.

Monuments are lit up by Fourth of July fireworks.

People can travel to and from the city by car and plane.

Fish from the Chesapeake Bay are sold in the city.

VISITOR'S MAP

White House

Washington Monument

Capitol

Jefferson Memorial

North
West East

MAP KEY

Building   Parking

Using maps helps us to find out how to get to where we want to go.

Signs help us find places like the White House.

PENNSYLVANIA AV NW
1600

Using Maps

Words to Know

map
symbol
map key
country
state

Look at the photograph on this page. It shows what a neighborhood looks like from above.

A **map** is a drawing of a place. The map on the next page is a drawing of the same neighborhood. How are the picture and map alike?

H9

Maps can have **symbols**. A symbol is something that stands for something else.

Maps also have a **map key**. Map keys tell what the symbols on a map mean.

 How is a map key useful?

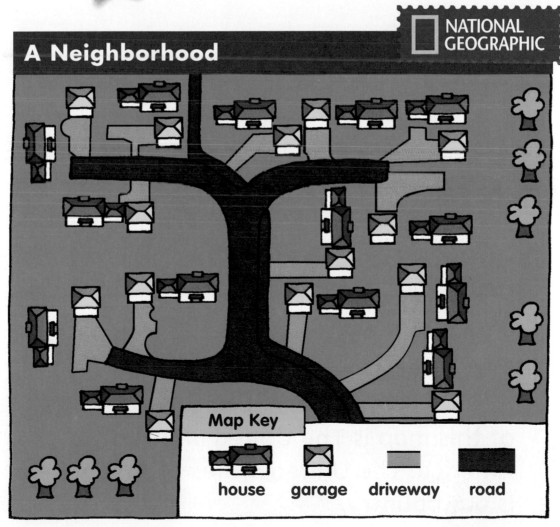

A Neighborhood

Map Key

house   garage   driveway   road

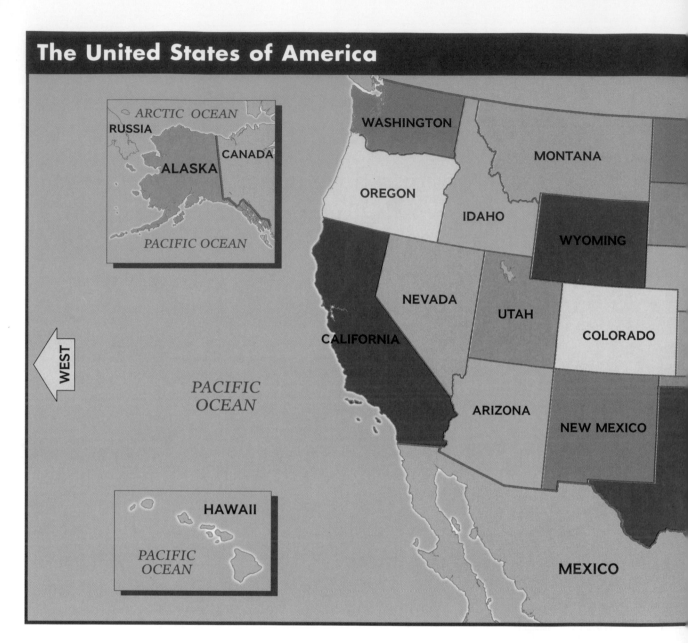

The United States of America

ARCTIC OCEAN
RUSSIA
CANADA
ALASKA
PACIFIC OCEAN

WASHINGTON
MONTANA
OREGON
IDAHO
WYOMING
NEVADA
UTAH
COLORADO
CALIFORNIA
WEST
PACIFIC OCEAN
ARIZONA
NEW MEXICO
HAWAII
PACIFIC OCEAN
MEXICO

Our Country

Most maps have titles. The title
tells you what the map shows. The title
of this map is The United States of
America. The United States of America
is our **country**.

A country is a land and the people who live there. Our country is made up of fifty **states**. A state is a part of a country.

 Which states touch your state?

Using Globes

Words to Know

globe
continent
ocean
direction

A **globe** is a model of Earth. A model is a copy of something.

Globes show the **continents**. A continent is a very large body of land. Earth has seven continents.

Globes also show **oceans**. An ocean is a very large body of salt water. Earth has four oceans.

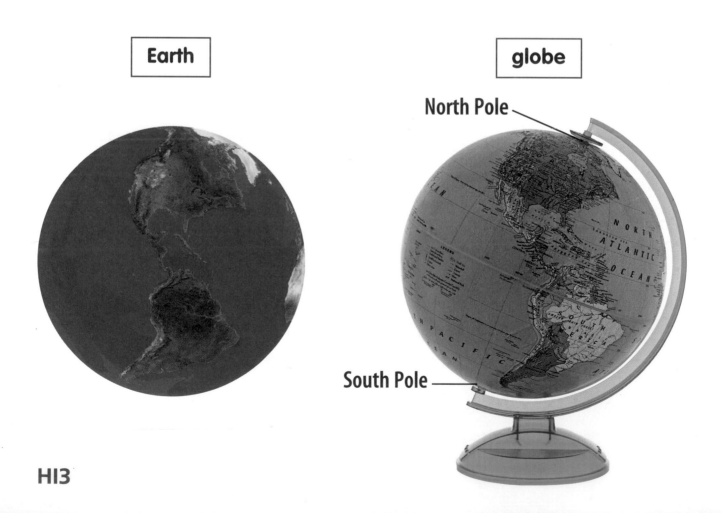

Earth

globe

North Pole

South Pole

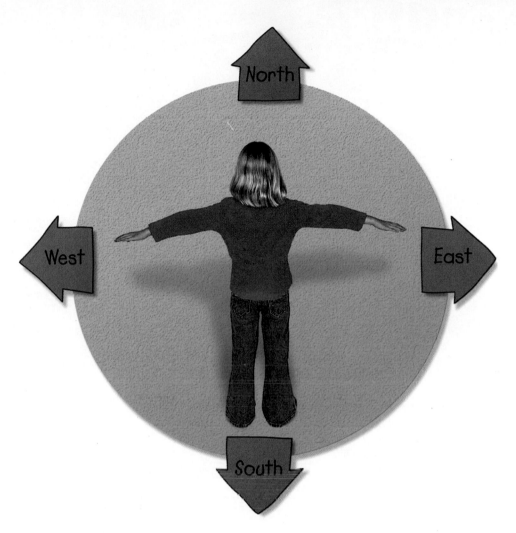

Using Directions

A **direction** is any way you can face or point. There are four main directions. They are north, south, east, and west. Directions help us answer the question, "Where is it?"

 What direction is the girl facing?

Literature

Helping Hands

by Gene Duerk

illustrated by William Low

The storm left water everywhere! Our house was flooded. Mom and I had to leave.

Our friends helped us.

Mom and I went to the school. We needed food and dry clothing. We needed a place to sleep for the night.

Our friends helped us.

Mom and I got up early the next day. There was so much to do! We needed to fix our house.

Our friends helped us.

Today, Mom and I move back into our house. We say *thank you* to our friends.

One day, we hope to help them.

Talk about it!

How did the community help?

Our Community

These children live in a big city. What do you know about where you live?

Explore more about
communities at our Web site
www.mhschool.com

What Is a Community?

A **community** is a place where people live, work, and have fun together. Read what Kevin says about his community.

"Portsmouth, New Hampshire, is where we live."

"I go with my family to the community fair."

"Dad delivers mail to people in my community."

Everyone lives in a community. In this unit you will learn about different kinds of communities.

9

Words to Know

About Communities

Find the pictures and say the words.

neighbors

museum

transportation

law

10

Talk about it!

What do you see in this picture?

Living in a Community

Words to Know

neighbors
museum

People live in communities. Some people live close to each other. They are called **neighbors**. Neighbors live together in a neighborhood.

Kyle's Apartment

Kyle

Ann Arbor, MICHIGAN

Joe and Kyle live in Ann Arbor, Michigan. Kyle lives in an apartment. Kyle's friend Joe lives in a house. They are neighbors.

What are neighbors?

Joe's House

Joe

Places in Our Community

Today Joe and Kyle are meeting their friend, Julie. Joe and Kyle live in one neighborhood. Julie lives in another neighborhood. But they all live in the same community! They all live in Ann Arbor.

Joe and Kyle's neighborhood

Joe, Kyle, and Julie are meeting at the Hands-On **Museum**. A museum is a place that keeps things for people to see and learn about. Today, they will learn how a hot air balloon works.

Hands-On Museum

Julie's neighborhood

What is a museum?

15

West Park

Downtown Ann Arbor

North Main St.

West Huron St.

Sharing Our Community

There are many other things to do in Ann Arbor. In West Park you can skate, hike, hear music, and play tennis and baseball.

Some people in Ann Arbor go to community meetings at City Hall. They talk about ways to make community life better for everyone.

City Hall

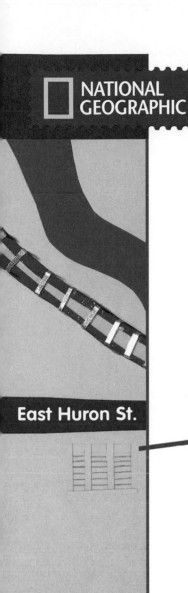

East Huron St.

Power Center

At the Power Center you can hear music and see plays. Joe likes to go there with his mom and dad to see a play.

What things can you do in Ann Arbor?

Think and Write!

1. How does a community meeting help the community?

2. What things can you do in your community?

17

Problem Solving

A **problem** is something you need to think about. You **solve** a problem when you find an answer to it. There are three steps to solving a problem.

Step 1: Name the problem.

Ann has a problem. She is at school. She left her homework at a neighbor's house.

Step 2: List different choices.

Ann could go to her neighbor's house to get the homework. Ann could call her dad and ask him to go to the neighbor's house. Ann could tell her teacher what happened and ask to do the homework again at recess.

Step 3: Think and solve the problem.

Ann does not have time to go to her neighbor's house. Her dad is busy at work. So, Ann will tell her teacher and ask to do the homework again at recess.

Try The Skill

1. What is the first step in solving a problem?

2. Why is it a good idea to list different choices?

3. What did Ann do to solve her problem?

From City to Country

There are many different kinds of communities. One kind of community is an **urban area**. An urban area is a city and the places around it.

Words to Know

urban area
suburb
rural area

Norfolk, Virginia, is an urban area. It has tall buildings where many people work and shop. Cars, trucks, and buses make the streets very busy.

Norfolk is near the water. Large ships come and go every day.

What can you see in a city?

Near the City

A **suburb** is another kind of community. A suburb is a community that is near a city. The word "suburb" is made out of two parts. The part "sub" means *near*. The part "urb" means *city*.

Larchmont, Virginia, is a suburb. It is near the city of Norfolk, Virginia. Many people live in Larchmont and travel to Norfolk every day for work.

Most suburbs are not as busy as cities. They have many open areas, like parks and fields.

 What is a suburb?

VIRGINIA

Larchmont

Smithfield

Norfolk

In the Country

A **rural area** is another kind of community. Rural areas are made up mostly of farmland. In rural areas, you can see more land than houses!

Smithfield, Virginia, is a town in a rural area. It has a main street with a post office and stores. People drive into Smithfield to go shopping.

OLD COURT HOUSE
BUILT IN 1750

SMITHFIELD VIRGINIA
INCORPORATED 175?

Smithfield also has a courthouse. It is the oldest building in Smithfield. People in Smithfield made the courthouse a symbol of their town. Today it is a museum.

 What is a rural area?

Think and Write!

1. **What did the people of Smithfield choose for their town symbol?**

2. **Make a drawing of an *urban area*, *rural area*, or *suburb*.**

Celebrate Communities

with a Poem

Until We Built a Cabin

by Aileen Fisher

When we lived in a city
(three flights up and down)
I never dreamed how many stars
could show above a town.

When we moved to a village
where lighted streets were few,
I thought I could see ALL the stars,
but, oh, I never knew . . .

Until we built a cabin
where hills are high and far,
I never knew how many
many stars there really are.

Using a Compass Rose

Look at the map of Indiana on the next page. There is a special symbol on this map called a **compass rose** . A compass rose has arrows that point to the letters **N, S, E,** and **W.** These arrows show the directions north, south, east, and west.

Find the Wyandotte Cave on the map. Now find Fort Wayne. Look at the compass rose. It shows you that Wyandotte Cave is south of Fort Wayne.

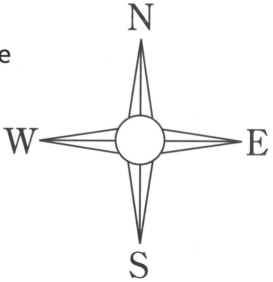

Try The Skill

1. Is the Children's Museum of Indianapolis north or south of Wyandotte Cave?

2. Is the Indiana Dunes State Park east or west of Fort Wayne?

Indiana

Indiana Dunes
State Park

Fort
Wayne

Wabash River

Children's
Museum of
Indianapolis

INDIANA

White River

Wyandotte
Cave

N
W — E
S

Make It! Make a map of your classroom.
Use a compass rose to show
north, south, east, and west.

Changing Communities

Life in communities has changed over the years. One of those changes is in **transportation**. Transportation is a way of moving people or things from one place to another.

Words to Know

transportation
communication

Years ago many people rode streetcars. Horses pulled the first streetcars.

Today, most people use cars for transportation. Henry Ford was one of the first people to make a car. He called his car a Model T. He found a way to make lots of Model Ts very quickly. Many families bought these cars.

Henry Ford standing by his Model T

 Name one kind of transportation used long ago. Name one used today.

Communication Then and Now

Long ago, communication was very slow and difficult. Communication is the way people share ideas, thoughts, or information with each other.

In those days, there were no telephones. People sent letters. It could take weeks for a letter to get from one community to another!

Today, we have telephones. People can carry telephones in their pockets and make calls from wherever they are!

Many people also use computers to communicate. They send e-mails or *electronic mail* from one computer to another.

 How did people communicate long ago?

Community Fun

How did people in communities have fun long ago? Well, there were no televisions or computers then. In the winter, people ice-skated outside on ponds or lakes. In the summer, they swam in the lakes, ponds, or oceans.

Today, people play games on their computers. They can ice-skate all year long in indoor rinks. People can still swim in lakes, ponds, and oceans. But, they also can swim in heated pools all year long.

A few things have not changed. Today, families still enjoy spending time together just like they did long ago.

 How has having fun changed?

Think and Write!

1. Name something that is the same today as it was long ago.

2. Make a chart titled "past" and "present." List different kinds of transportation, communication, and ways of having fun.

Lesson 4

Getting Along

Words to Know

law

citizen

People in communities need to get along with one another. Rules help people get along. Rules tell us what to do and what not to do.

36

You follow rules in your classroom. Following the rules makes the classroom a better place.

Community rules are called **laws**. Laws are rules we must all follow. Laws keep a community clean and safe. They make a community a better place.

 Why should you follow rules and laws?

Good Citizens

Following laws is an important part of being a good **citizen**. A citizen is a member of a community, state, or country.

Another way to be a good citizen is to help others. Mark helps his neighbor put her groceries into her car.

We can keep our community beautiful. We can plant flowers, rake leaves, and keep our community clean.

A good citizen follows rules and helps others. This makes the community a better place to live.

 What does a good citizen do?

Think and Write!

1 How are you a good citizen?

2 How do rules help us?

Biography

Jane Addams

Jane Addams thought it was important to help others. About 100 years ago, she opened a community center in Chicago, Illinois. She named it Hull-House. At Hull-House, she cared for children of working parents.

Read what Jane Addams said about all people.

In her own words

> **"All the people in the world are neighbors. Hull-House taught me that."**
> —Jane Addams

Jane cared about keeping the streets of Chicago clean. She got the city to pick up garbage. She also helped women get the right to vote.

Explore more about the life of Jane Addams at our Web site www.mhschool.com

Being a Good Citizen
The Kids for Kids Cookbook

Chelsea Rae Chambers lives in Potsdam, New York. One day, Chelsea read a story about collecting money to buy school supplies for needy families.

Chelsea had an idea. She would make a cookbook. Then she could sell her cookbook to make money for the school supplies program!

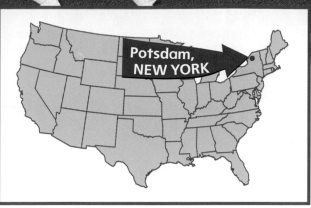

Potsdam, NEW YORK

Chelsea made a cookbook filled with recipes from family, friends, and classmates. Chelsea raised $1,000!

Although making the cookbook was hard work, Chelsea didn't mind. "It made me feel good to know I was helping kids start the school year off right."

Chelsea Rae Chambers

KIDS
FOR
KIDS
COOKBOOK

by Chelsea Rae Chambers
To benefit the Church & Community
Worker's Back to School Supplies
Program

Be a Good Citizen

What are some ways people in your community help others?

Activity

Talk about a problem in your community. Make a plan for how you and your classmates can help.

Using Calendars

A **calendar** is a chart that shows the 12 months of the year. It also shows the number of days in each month and the seven days of the week.

Look at the community calendar page for the month of May. Find the number 6. May 6th is on a Tuesday. What happened on that day?

Try The Skill

1. What day of the week is Clean Up the Park Day?

2. How many days long is the County Fair?

 **Make It!** Make a special calendar for your birthday month.

May

Sunday	Monday	Tuesday	Wednesday	Thursday	Friday	Saturday
				1	2	3
4	5	6 Library Book Sale	7	8	9	10 Clean Up the Park Day
11	12	13	14	15	16 County Fair	17 County Fair
18 County Fair	19	20	21	22	23	24
25 Bicycle Race	26 Memorial Day	27	28	29	30	31

A Story About a Community

Words to Know

interview
legend

David lives in El Paso, Texas. He wanted to learn what life was like in his community long ago. His neighbor, Mrs. Garza, gave him a book to read about El Paso.

Look at the chart on the next page. It tells you things about El Paso that you will learn in this lesson.

El Paso, TEXAS

El Camino Real

Mexico City, MEXICO

El Paso Long Ago and Today

Long Ago	Today
There was a Thanksgiving celebration held in April 1598.	There are two Thanksgiving celebrations. One is in April and one is in November.
There was a path from Mexico City to Texas, called El Camino Real. It passed through El Paso.	The El Camino Real path is now a road. The part that passes through El Paso is called Highway I-10.
People traveled on foot, by horse, and by wagon.	People travel by car.

Chart Skill

What kind of transportation did people use long ago?

 How does David learn about El Paso?

47

Interview a Neighbor

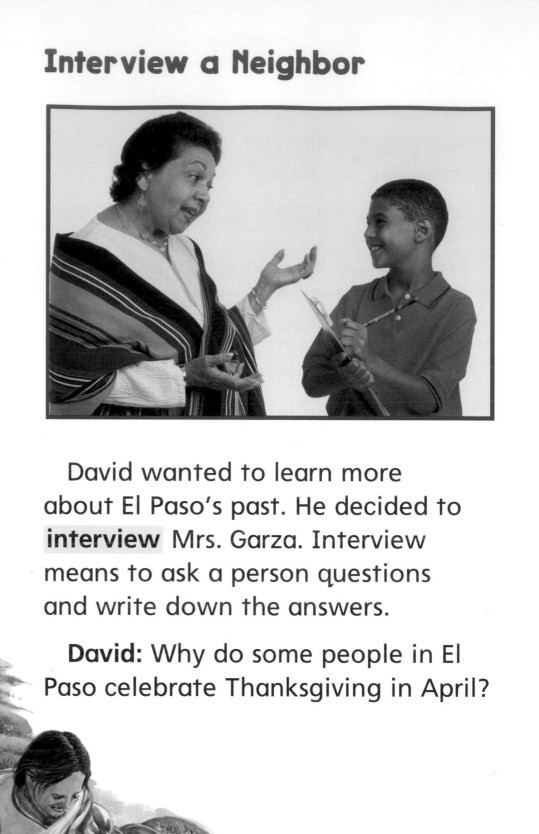

David wanted to learn more about El Paso's past. He decided to **interview** Mrs. Garza. Interview means to ask a person questions and write down the answers.

David: Why do some people in El Paso celebrate Thanksgiving in April?

Mrs. Garza: One April, long ago, people from Mexico traveled north along a path called the El Camino Real. The path passed through a hot, dry desert. Many died because there was no water to drink. When they saw a river called the Rio Grande, they were so happy. Some say this was our country's first Thanksgiving.

David: What do El Camino Real and Rio Grande mean in English?

Mrs. Garza: In English, El Camino Real is *The Royal Road.* The Rio Grande is *Great River*.

Why were people so happy to reach the Rio Grande?

An El Paso Legend

David: Can you tell me the story of the bluebonnet?

Mrs. Garza: It is a very old legend. A legend is a story that has been told for many years.

Long, long ago this land was very dry. A Wise Man told the people "The Great Spirit is not happy. It will not rain until you give the thing you love most back to Earth."

A little girl had a doll she loved very much. It had blue feathers on its head. That night she went to the campfire. She told the Great Spirit to take her doll. Then she put her doll in the fire.

50

After the fire died down, she threw the ashes everywhere. The next morning, the ground was covered with flowers. They were as blue as the feathers from the doll's head.

Now, every spring, the hills of Texas are covered with the blue flowers—bluebonnets!

David: That is a great story! Thanks, Mrs. Garza.

 What is a legend?

Think and Write!

1. What does David learn from his interview with Mrs. Garza?

2. How could you learn about your community's history?

A Look at a Community in Senegal

Kaolack is an urban community in the country of Senegal. Senegal is on the continent of Africa.

It is very warm in Kaolack. The people dress in light, bright clothes.

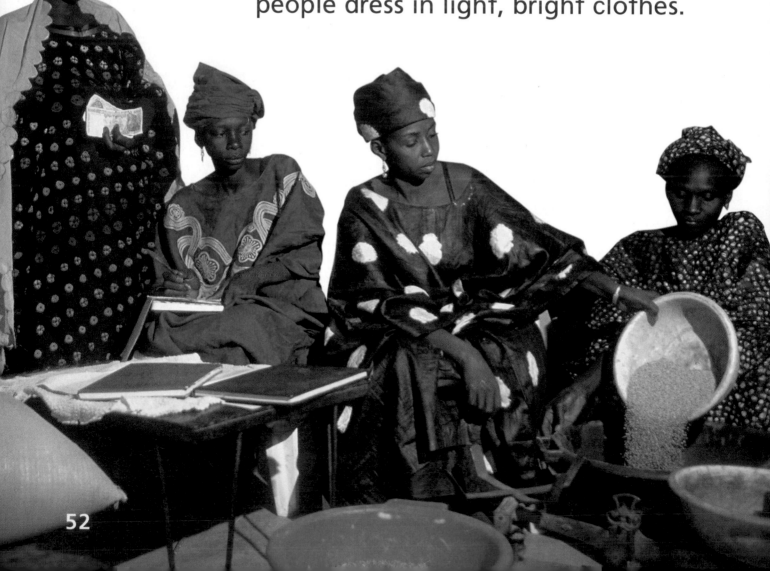

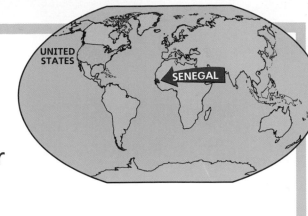

The people in Kaolack enjoy seeing artwork at their beautiful community center. The community center also has an outside theater where people can come to watch plays and shows.

Kaolack's Community Center

Talk about it!

How is Kaolack like other communities you have learned about?

Words to Know

Choose the word that best completes each sentence.

transportation   community   law

1. A place where people live, work, and have fun together is a _____ .

2. A _____ is a rule we must all follow.

3. A way of moving people from one place to another is called _____ .

Check Your Reading

4. Name some ways we can communicate with each other.

5. How has transportation changed from long ago?

6. Name three types of communities. How are they alike?

Use a Calendar

7. What happened on June 15?

8. What day of the week is Dean's birthday?

June

Sunday	Monday	Tuesday	Wednesday	Thursday	Friday	Saturday
1 Dean's Birthday	2	3	4	5	6 Last Day of School	7
8	9	10	11	12	13	14
15 Father's Day	16	17	18	19	20	21
22	23	24	25	26	27	28
29	30					

 Make a calendar for next month.

55

Problem Solving

9. Billy was walking home from school. He saw Mrs. Smith. Her cat could not climb down from a tree. Mrs. Smith asked Billy to go get help.

Which picture shows the solution?

Use a Compass Rose

10. Radnor Lake, in the state of Tennessee, is a place to have fun. Is it north or south of the Capitol Building in Nashville?

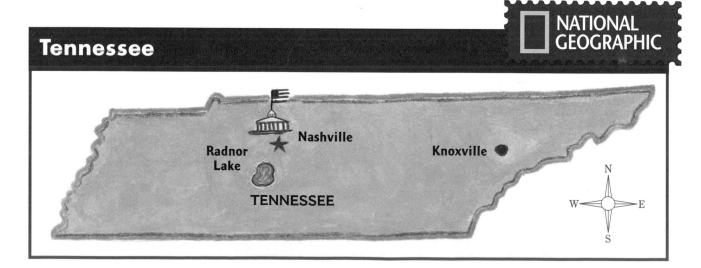

Tennessee

NATIONAL GEOGRAPHIC

Nashville
Radnor Lake
TENNESSEE
Knoxville

Activity

Postcard of Your Community

* Draw a picture on one side of an index card to show something in your community.

* On the other side, write a letter to someone that tells about your community.

Dear Sarah,
My community has a new bridge. My dad drives his truck across the bridge everyday.
Your friend,
Darien

Sarah Jones
176 Woodside Ave
Ft Lee, New Jersey
07653

Think and Write

Suppose you are riding a bike through your community. Write about what you see.

For more information about this unit, visit our Web site at **www.mhschool.com**

Literature

The Treasure Hunt

by Becky Manfredini and Jenny Reznick
illustrated by Obadinah Heavner

It's time for a treasure hunt.
Here's what to do.
Follow the trail.
It's up to you!

Walk over two hills.
Walk onto flat land.
Now board the train.
I will give you a hand!

First take the train
to the water so blue.
Now ride in the boat.
Please row the boat, too!

Row and row
until you see land.
Ahoy! There's a palm tree
beyond the gold sand.

Follow the trail
to the tallest palm tree.
The treasure is here.
Now dig with me!

Dig and dig
until you find the chest.
It's filled with treasure.
Now let's take a rest!

Talk about it!

What kinds of places
did the children see?

63

All About Earth

This is a picture of Earth. Can you tell what part is land? What part is water?

Explore Earth at our Web
site **www.mhschool.com**

65

How Does Geography Help Me?

Geography tells about Earth. It also tells about the people, plants, and animals that live on Earth. Read what Hannah says about geography.

"I use a globe to learn about the land and water that make up Earth."

"A map helps me find
my way around."

"I look at photographs to
see how places are alike
and different."

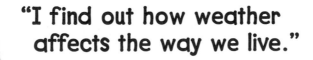

"I find out how weather
affects the way we live."

In this unit you will use maps,
globes, and photographs. You will
find out how geography helps you
understand more about our Earth.
You will learn about the people,
animals, and plants that live on Earth.

Words to Know
About Geography

Find the pictures and say the words.

island

peninsula

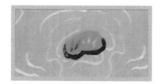

mountain

lake

Talk about it!

What do you see in this picture?

69

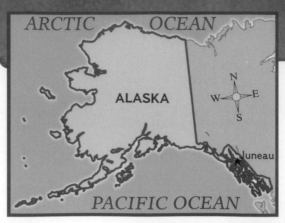

Where We Live

Meet Jamal. Jamal lives in Salem. It is the **capital** of Oregon. A capital is a city where leaders of a country or state work.

Oregon is a state.

Oregon

70

Oregon is a state. A state is one part of our country. Our country is called the United States of America. It is made up of 50 states.

NATIONAL GEOGRAPHIC

The United States of America

★ National capital   ★ State capital

Map Skill

Which states touch Oregon?

What is a capital?

Countries Have Neighbors

Countries have neighbors. Mexico is a country. Mexico and the United States are neighbors. Mexico is our neighbor to the south.

Canada is also a country. Canada is our neighbor to the north.

Our country is the United States.

United States

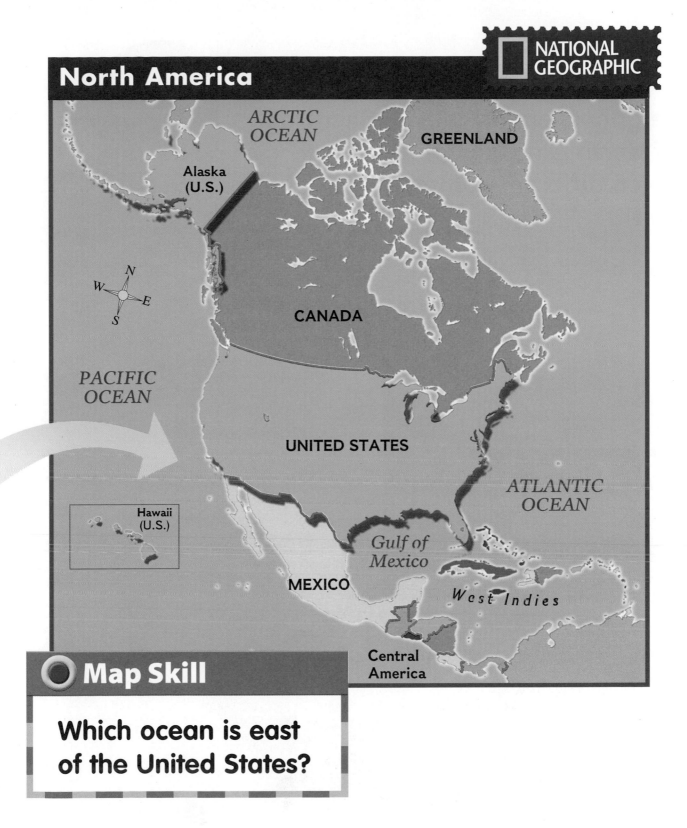

North America

NATIONAL GEOGRAPHIC

ARCTIC OCEAN

GREENLAND

Alaska (U.S.)

CANADA

PACIFIC OCEAN

UNITED STATES

Hawaii (U.S.)

ATLANTIC OCEAN

Gulf of Mexico

MEXICO

West Indies

Central America

⦿ Map Skill

Which ocean is east of the United States?

 Which countries are our neighbors?

73

Our World

The United States and its neighbors are on the continent of North America. There are seven different continents on Earth.

Can you find North America on the map?

The World

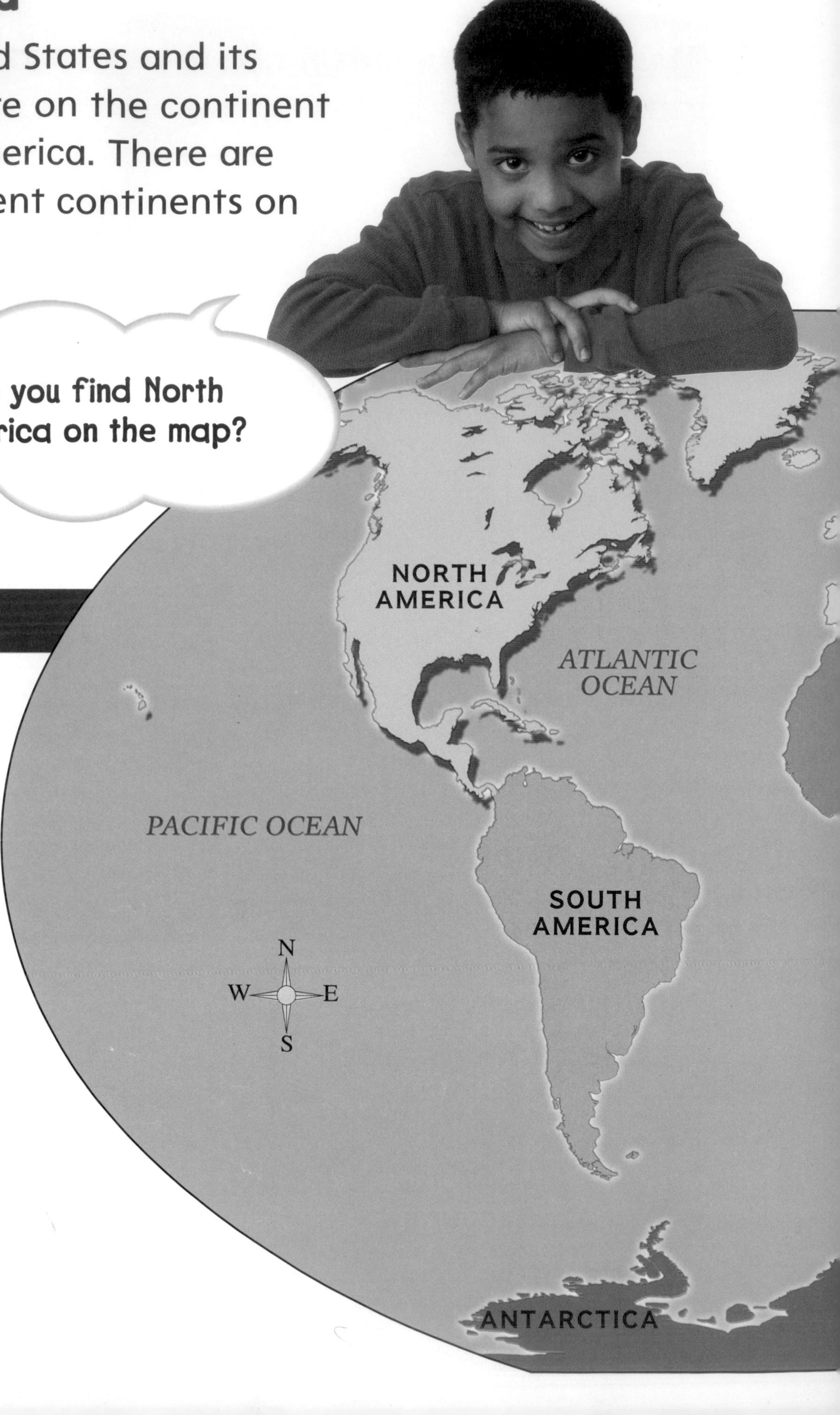

NORTH AMERICA

ATLANTIC OCEAN

PACIFIC OCEAN

N
W   E
S

SOUTH AMERICA

ANTARCTICA

The seven continents make up the land on Earth. The rest of Earth is made up of water.

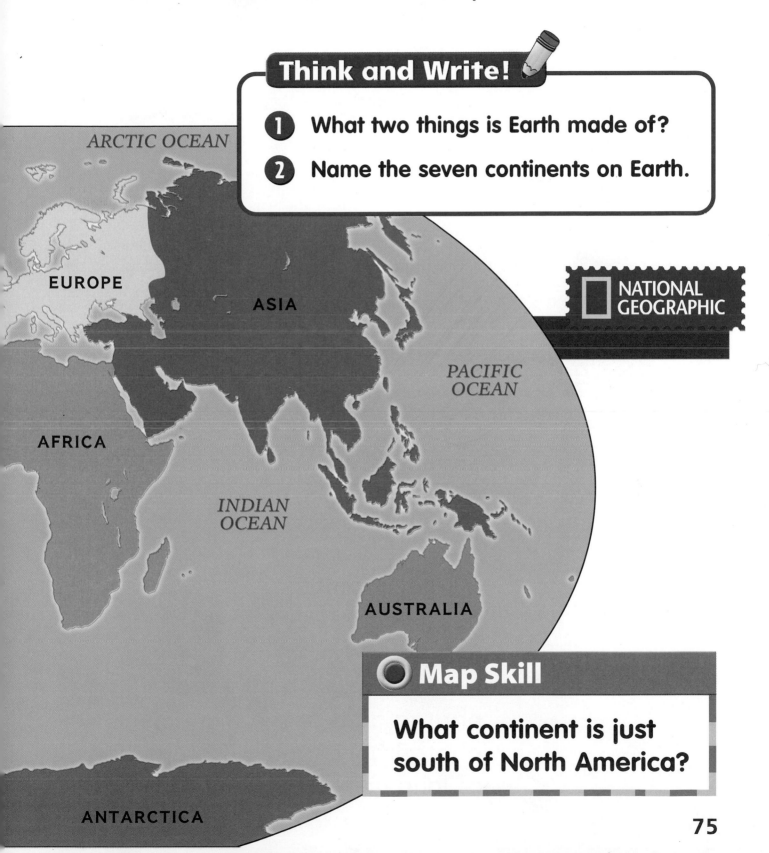

ARCTIC OCEAN

EUROPE

ASIA

AFRICA

PACIFIC
OCEAN

INDIAN
OCEAN

AUSTRALIA

ANTARCTICA

Think and Write!

1 What two things is Earth made of?

2 Name the seven continents on Earth.

☐ NATIONAL GEOGRAPHIC

◉ Map Skill

What continent is just south of North America?

Lesson 2

Land and Water

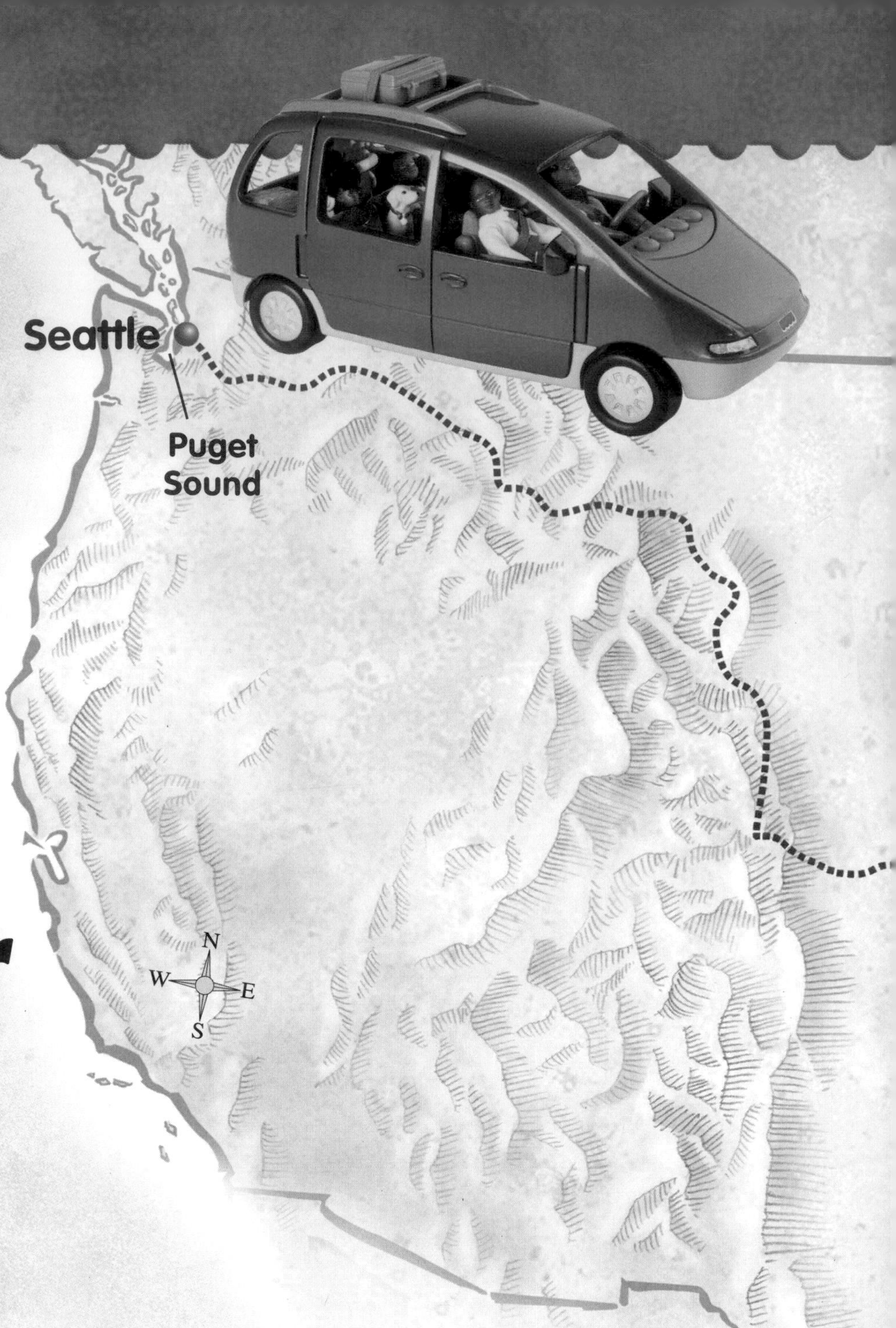
Seattle
Puget Sound
N
W
E
S

Words to Know

- landform
- island
- peninsula
- hill
- mountain
- valley
- plain
- lake
- river

Emily's family has moved. They drove from Seattle, Washington, to Wichita, Kansas. Emily's family took photographs of the trip. The photographs show different kinds of land and water.

"This island in Puget Sound is near my old home in Seattle."

"When we left, we drove past this beautiful peninsula."

 Wichita

There are different shapes of land on Earth. These different shapes are called **landforms**. A landform that has water going all the way around it is called an **island**. A landform that has water on all sides but one is called a **peninsula**.

What is the name of the landform that has water all around it?

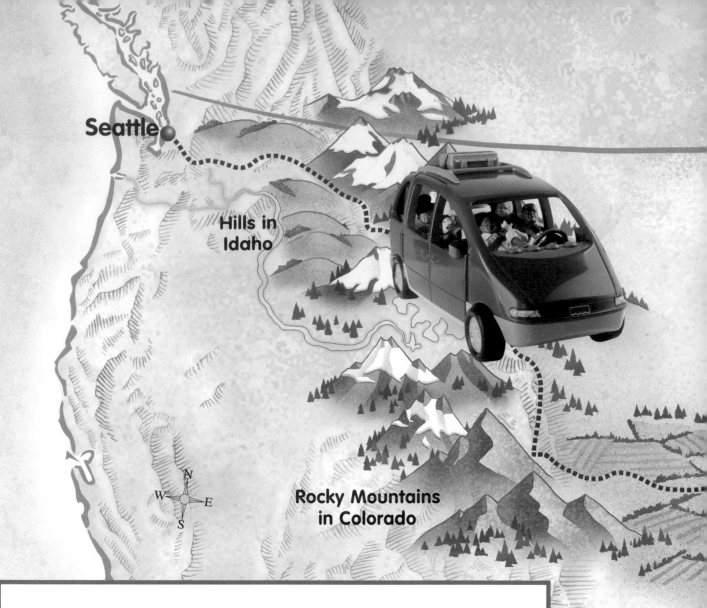

Seattle

Hills in
Idaho

Rocky Mountains
in Colorado

N
W   E
S

Kinds of Land

Hills and **mountains** are landforms. Both are high areas of land. A mountain is the highest form of land. A hill is higher than the land around it, but not as high as a mountain. The low area between mountains or hills is called a **valley**.

Some land is not high or low. It is flat. A flat area of land is called a **plain**.

"We drove past lots of hills in Idaho."

Plains in Kansas

● Wichita

"In Colorado we drove through a valley in the Rocky Mountains!"

"We saw plains when we reached the state of Kansas."

 Name four landforms.

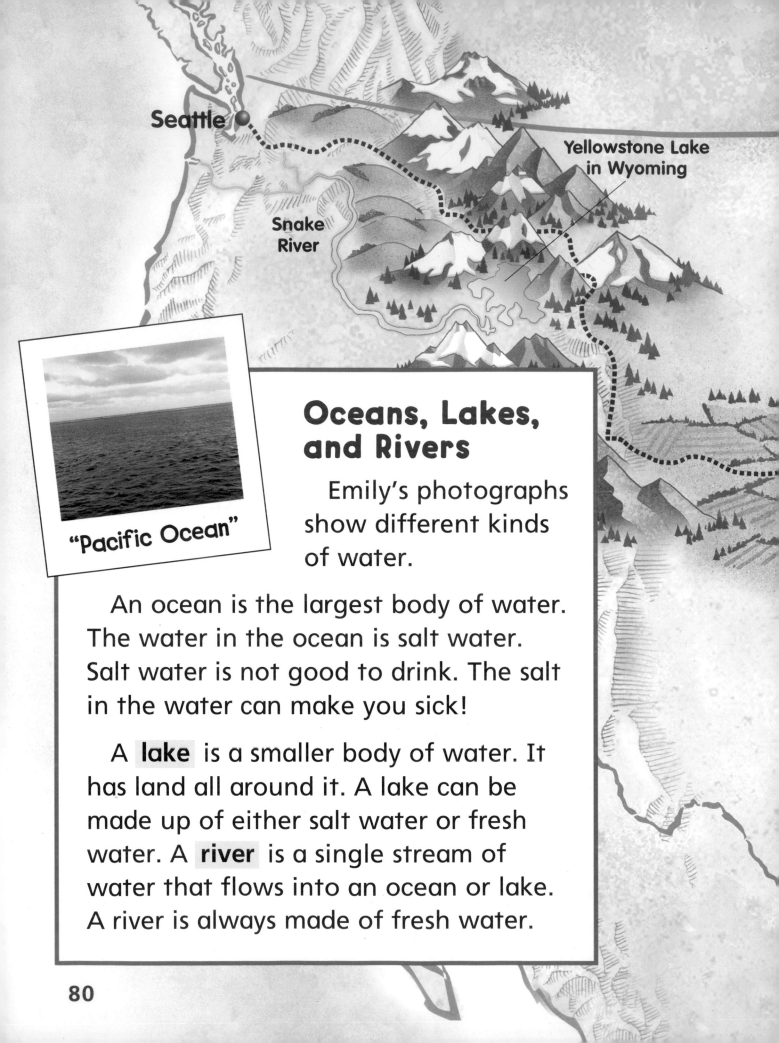

Seattle

Yellowstone Lake
in Wyoming

Snake
River

"Pacific Ocean"

Oceans, Lakes, and Rivers

Emily's photographs show different kinds of water.

An ocean is the largest body of water. The water in the ocean is salt water. Salt water is not good to drink. The salt in the water can make you sick!

A **lake** is a smaller body of water. It has land all around it. A lake can be made up of either salt water or fresh water. A **river** is a single stream of water that flows into an ocean or lake. A river is always made of fresh water.

"The Snake River twists and turns like a snake!"

"I saw Yellowstone Lake in Wyoming."

● Wichita

 Why is salt water not good to drink?

Think and Write! ✏️

1 What are the largest bodies of water called?

2 What is the difference between a mountain and a hill?

81

Celebrate America's Beauty

with a Song

Over 100 years ago, Katharine Lee Bates traveled to Pike's Peak, Colorado. She said, "When I saw the view, I felt great joy." She wrote about what she saw. Her words became the song *America, the Beautiful.*

America, the Beautiful

Words by Katharine Lee Bates *Music by Samuel Ward*

O beau - ti - ful for spa - cious skies, For am - ber waves of grain.

For pur - ple moun - tain maj - es - ties, A - bove the fruit - ed plain.

A - mer - i - ca! A - mer - i - ca! God shed His grace on thee,

And crown thy good with broth - er - hood, From sea to shin - ing sea.

Using Landform Maps

There is a special map that shows landforms. It is called a landform map. Landform maps use colors to show different kinds of land.

Look at the pictures with the color squares on this page. What color stands for mountains? Hills? Plains? Now look at the landform map of Oklahoma on the next page. The map key at the bottom shows the colors used for each kind of landform. Use the map and map key to answer the questions.

Try The Skill

1. What three landforms does Oklahoma have?

2. Are there more plains or mountains in Oklahoma?

Orange shows mountains.

Gold shows hills.

Green shows plains.

NATIONAL GEOGRAPHIC

Oklahoma Landforms

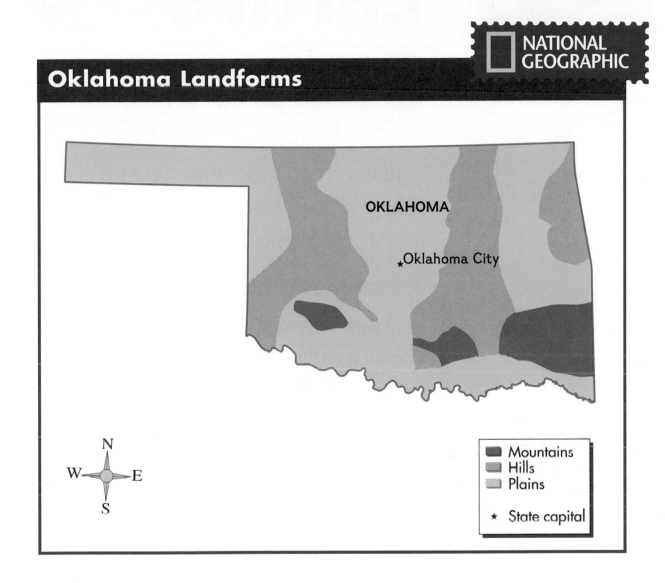

OKLAHOMA

★Oklahoma City

N
W—E
S

Legend:
- Mountains
- Hills
- Plains
- ★ State capital

Make It! Make a landform map of your home state.

85

Earth's Seasons

Words to Know

season

Milo lives in Pennsylvania. "When the weather is nice, I like to play outside," he says.

When we talk about rain or snow or how hot or cold it is, we are talking about the weather. Weather changes. "Yesterday it was rainy," says Milo. "Today it is sunny."

Weather is different from place to place. It may be snowing in Pennsylvania. At the same time it may be sunny in California.

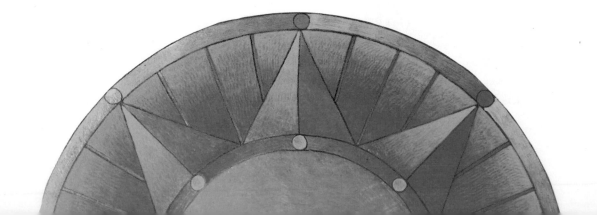

Some kinds of weather happen more often during a certain **season**. A season is a time of the year. There are four seasons. They are spring, summer, fall, and winter.

Spring

Summer

Fall

Winter

What kinds of weather can you name?

How Weather Affects Our Lives

Amanda lives in Florida. "People who don't like cold winters come to visit us." says Amanda. "I like Florida! It is warm here most of the year."

"Sometimes, though, we have big storms," says Amanda. "In our house, we have special covers on our windows. They keep out the rain and wind."

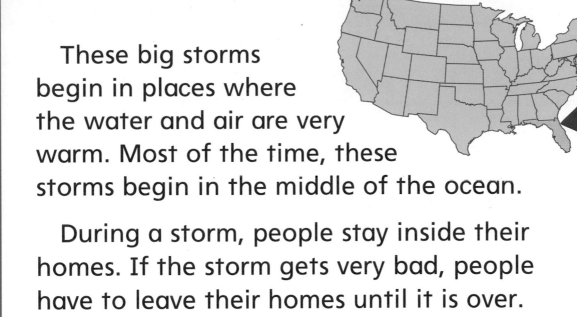

Florida

These big storms begin in places where the water and air are very warm. Most of the time, these storms begin in the middle of the ocean.

During a storm, people stay inside their homes. If the storm gets very bad, people have to leave their homes until it is over.

Why do some people like to visit Florida in the winter?

Think and Write!

1. How is the weather in Pennsylvania and Florida different?

2. Describe what happens when Florida has a storm.

89

Using Bar Graphs

A **bar graph** is a graph that uses bars to show and compare information.

This bar graph shows how many inches of rainfall the city of San Francisco gets each season.

Move your finger up the bar for Spring. It ends at the number 5. That means San Francisco usually has about 5 inches of rainfall in the spring.

Try The Skill

1. Which other season has 5 inches of rainfall?

2. Which season has the most rainfall?

 **Make It!** Make a bar graph of weather in your community for one week.

San Francisco Rainfall

Inches

	Winter	Spring	Summer	Fall
10				
9				
8				
7				
6				
5				
4				
3				
2				
1				
0				

Earth's Resources

Words to Know

natural resources

A resource is something that is ready to use. Nature is full of things that are ready for people to use. We call these things **natural resources**.

The most important natural resources we have are air, water, sunlight, and soil. Without them, we would not be able to breathe, drink, see, or grow food!

Name two natural resources.

Building with Natural Resources

People use natural resources for many things. Trees can be used to build houses. They can also be used to make chairs.

Sand is also a natural resource. Did you know that glass is made from sand? The sand is heated and mixed with other things. Then, it is poured into molds until it becomes cool and dry.

The chart on the next page shows you some things that are made from natural resources.

Natural Resources and Things Made From Them

Corn	**Cornmeal**	**Popcorn**	**Corn Oil**
Trees	**Paper**	**Table**	**Syrup**
Sand	**Cement**	**Sandpaper**	**Glass**
Iron	**Pipes**	**Cans**	**Tools**

○ Chart Skill

Cans and pipes are made from what natural resource?

Think and Write!

1. What is a natural resource?

2. Why are air, water, sunlight, and soil so important?

People Change Earth

People change Earth every day. We cut down trees to build homes. We move soil to build roads. We build dams across rivers to hold the water. We dig in the ground to find coal and oil to heat our homes.

 Name two ways people change Earth.

Hoover Dam

Pumping for oil

Changing the Soil

Changing Earth can help people get more out of natural resources. Some areas have good soil, but not enough rain to keep the soil wet. The farmers in these areas use special machines to put water into the soil.

Watering the soil

Some areas have enough water, but the soil is not good. Farmers make the soil better by mixing it with special plant food.

What do farmers do if the soil is good but there is no rain?

Think and Write!

1 Name two natural resources that we use to heat our homes.

2 Why do people change the land?

Putting Things in Order

You can show the order of when something happened first, next, and last. This is called putting things in order by time.

Look at the pictures below. They are in time order. The first picture shows corn before it is cooked. The next shows a piece of cooked corn. The last picture shows that the corn has been eaten.

First   Next   Last

(a)

(b)

(c)

Look at each of the three pictures. They are not in order. Now answer the questions.

Try The Skill

1. Which picture comes first? Next? Last?

2. What do these pictures show?

3. Why is it important to know the order in which things happen?

Protecting Earth

Earth is our home. We must be careful not to harm it. We need it to be our home now and in the future. Future means the time that is to come.

We need to be careful about the changes we make to Earth. Sometimes, the changes made cause problems.

Words to Know

recycle

If we cut too many trees, we might not have enough in the future. If we move water from one place to another, the first place can become too dry. Plants and animals there could die.

We should not waste our natural resources. That way we will have what we need in the future.

What changes could cause Earth problems?

You Can Help Earth

People can solve these problems in many ways. We keep our natural resources alive by planting. People can plant new trees to take the place of trees we have cut down.

We can save our natural resources by using less water. We can also **recycle**. When we recycle something, we use it again and again.

Many people recycle old newspapers, cans, bottles, and boxes. These things are then turned into something new. Can you think of some things you could recycle?

 What is recycling?

Think and Write!

1 Name two ways we can save natural resources.

2 Why is it important to protect our Earth?

105

Biography

John Muir

John Muir loved nature. He spent his life writing, drawing, and speaking about nature. His words made people care about Earth.

Read what John Muir wrote about how all things in nature work together.

In his own words

"When one tugs at a single thing in nature, he finds it attached to the rest of the world."

— *John Muir*

Once he went on a camping trip with President Theodore Roosevelt. He told the President how he felt about protecting nature. After the trip, President Roosevelt changed millions of acres of forests into public parks.

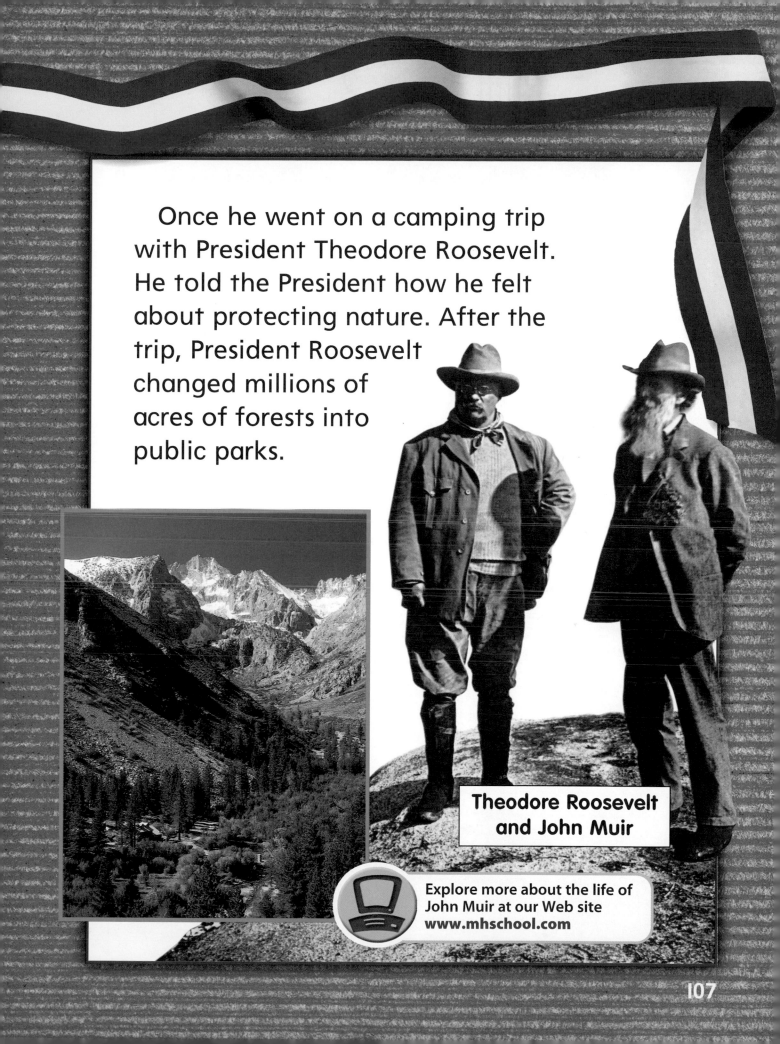

Theodore Roosevelt and John Muir

Explore more about the life of John Muir at our Web site www.mhschool.com

Making Decisions
Showing Respect

John Muir showed respect for nature. You show respect whenever you decide to honor other people, places, or things.

Read these stories. What decisions would you make?

I promised my mom that I would put away the dishes now.

You can do that later. Let's go out and play!

My sister left her diary on the table. Should I read it?

★ Be a Good Citizen

Why is it important to show respect? Ask your parents, teacher, or other adult.

Activity

Make a poster showing ways you could show respect in the classroom.

109

A Look at Brazil's Geography

The Amazon Rain Forest in Brazil is home to many plants and animals. It also gives the people of Brazil many natural resources.

These animals and plants would die if the Amazon Rain Forest was cut down. Many people are working hard to protect these animals and plants. They want to make sure that people use the Amazon Rain Forest wisely.

Talk about it!

Why is it important to protect the Amazon Rain Forest?

111

Words to Know

Choose the word that best completes each sentence.

| geography   mountain   peninsula |

1. The highest form of land is a ____.

2. Land that has water on all sides but one is called a ____ .

3. ____ tells you about Earth and the people, plants, and animals who live on Earth.

Check Your Reading

4. Which two countries border the United States?

5. Why are air, water, sunlight, and soil our most important natural resources?

6. How can we help Earth?

Use Bar Graphs

Use the bar graph below to answer the following questions.

7. How many cans were recycled?

8. How many boxes and bottles were recycled in all?

Number of Items

One Day of Recycling at Home

cans | magazines | bottles | boxes

Make It! Make a bar graph of the things you recycle at home.

113

Put Things in Order

9. Which picture comes first?

◯   ◯   ◯

Use Landform Maps

10. What landform is east of the hills?

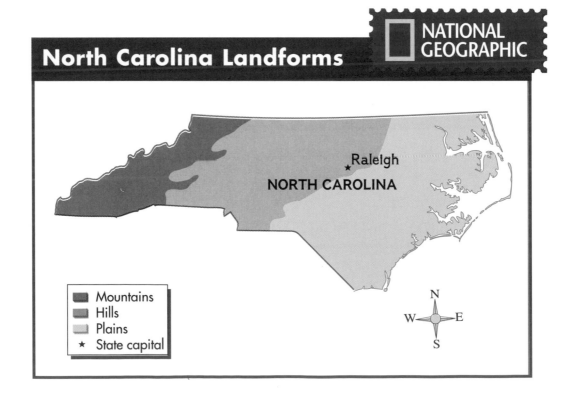

North Carolina Landforms

NATIONAL GEOGRAPHIC

★ Raleigh

NORTH CAROLINA

■ Mountains
■ Hills
■ Plains
★ State capital

N
W   E
S

Activity

Make a "Care for Earth" Poster

* Draw pictures of ways to help keep your community clean and safe.

* Label your pictures. Add them to your poster.

* Hang your poster on the classroom wall.

Think and Write

What could happen if we don't care about our Earth?

For more information about this unit, visit our Web site at **www.mhschool.com**

Literature

A Pilgrim Girl's Journal

by Mara Sands

illustrated by Lori Lohstoeter

September 16, 1620

Today we left England. Father says that we are going to build our new home in America. We are sailing on a ship called the *Mayflower*. I share a small corner of the ship with my family.

October 25, 1620

Our trip has been long and hard. The weather is cold and stormy. Sometimes I get seasick. My brother and I play to pass the time. Today we are having salted meat, peas, and beans for supper. I'm hungry!

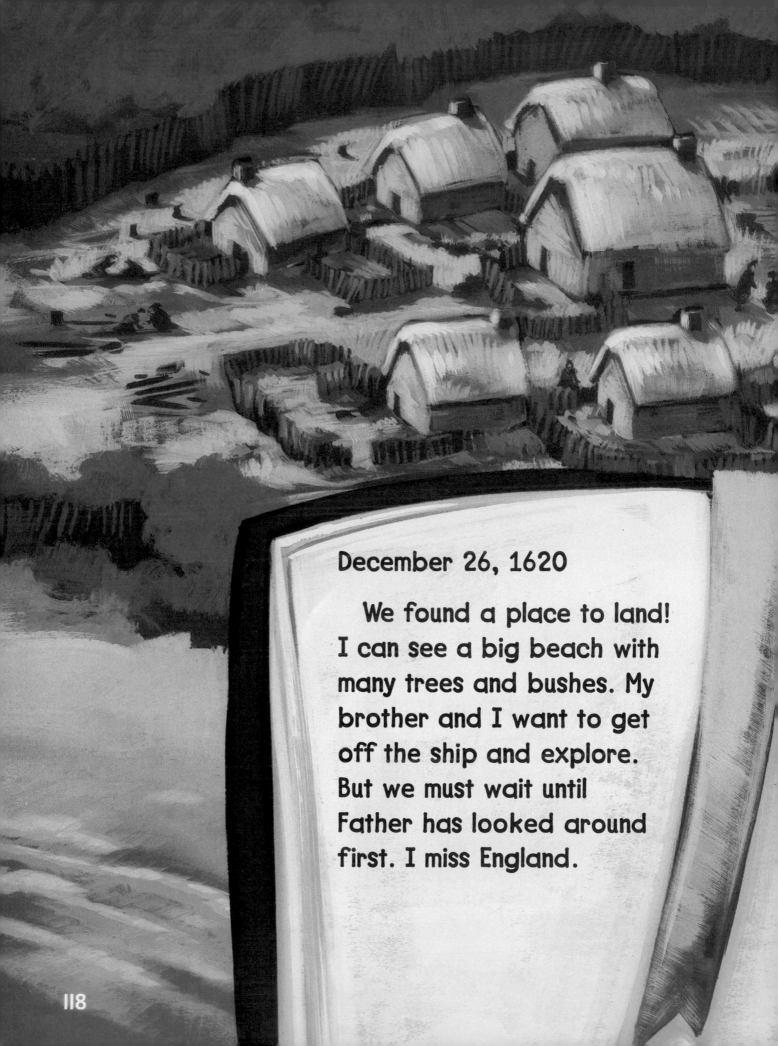

December 26, 1620

We found a place to land! I can see a big beach with many trees and bushes. My brother and I want to get off the ship and explore. But we must wait until Father has looked around first. I miss England.

March 28, 1621

My brother is helping Father chop wood to make a fire. Mother is washing our clothes. Yesterday we planted seeds in the garden. New friends have shown us how to grow fruits and vegetables. Now I like our new home in America.

Talk about it!

What would it be like if you left your country and moved far away?

Our Past

Long ago this family moved West to find a home. They traveled in a covered wagon. Why is it important to learn about our past?

Explore our country's
history at our Web site
www.mhschool.com

How Do I Learn About History?

There are many ways to learn about history. **History** is the story of the past. Read how Tracy learns about history.

"I read books about the past."

A FLAG FOR OUR COUNTRY

"I visit museums."

"I talk to people
in my community."

In this unit you will learn more about
the history of our country.

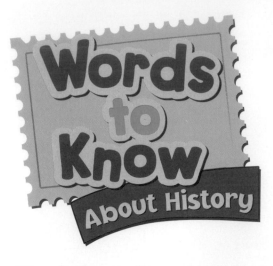

Words to Know

About History

Find the pictures and say the words.

Native Americans

explorers

pioneers

Talk about it!

What do you see in this picture?

America's First People

Words to Know

Native Americans
tradition

There are many groups of **Native Americans**. Native Americans were the first people to live in America. They are also called American Indians.

Look at the map on the next page. It shows where some Native American groups lived long ago. Each group had its own way of doing things. Groups had their own stories, songs, and music. The chart shows the homes and clothing of some of these groups.

What is another name for Native Americans?

Using Charts

Native American Groups

| Yurok | Lakota Sioux | Iroquois |
| Caddo | Navajo | Cherokee |

Chart Skill

In what way were the homes of Native American groups different?

The Yurok

Long ago, the Yurok lived in what is now the state of California. They used things from Earth, like roots, ferns, and sticks, to make strong baskets. They used trees to make canoes. Often, they traded the canoes with other groups of Native Americans.

Today, the Yurok still live in California. Children learn about Yurok **traditions** by talking to older Yurok members. A tradition is a special way of doing something that is passed down over time.

The Yurok follow many traditions. They make baskets, fish, dance, sing songs, and tell stories the same way as they did long ago.

 Do you think that it is important to follow traditions? Tell why.

Think and Write!

1 What kinds of things did the Yurok make?

2 What traditions do you follow?

Sorting into Groups

Sorting means putting things that are alike into groups. Look at the pictures of Native American things on this page.

Do you see the necklace? Now look at the other pictures that are like the necklace. Do you see the earrings and the bracelet? You could name this group, "Native American Jewelry."

Look at the other pictures. They are all shoes! You could name that group, "Native American Shoes."

 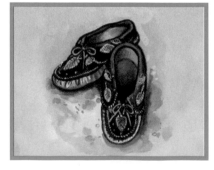 

Try The Skill

Here are six more pictures for you to sort.

1. Find the picture of the tepee. Now find two other pictures that are like the tepee. What could you name that group?

2. How are the other three pictures alike?

3. What could you name that group?

The Spanish Come to America

Native Americans were the first people to live in America. Many years later, **explorers** came from Europe. An explorer is a person who travels to a new place to learn about it.

One early explorer was Christopher Columbus. Columbus sailed from Spain to North America in 1492. He was the captain of three ships called the *Niña*, the *Pinta*, and the *Santa Maria*.

Columbus thought that he was sailing to the continent of Asia. He did not know that he had landed on North America. Native Americans called the Taino lived there. The Taino welcomed Columbus.

Who were the Taino?

Spanish Towns and Missions

After Columbus, other people from Spain came to live in America. One of the first towns the Spanish built is a town called St. Augustine. St. Augustine is in Florida.

Father Serra was a priest from Spain. He started many missions in California. A mission is a church or a place where a group of church members work.

Mission San Diego

St. Augustine

Native Americans were forced to work hard building the missions. Also, many became sick.

Spanish people built other towns and missions. Look at the map to find them.

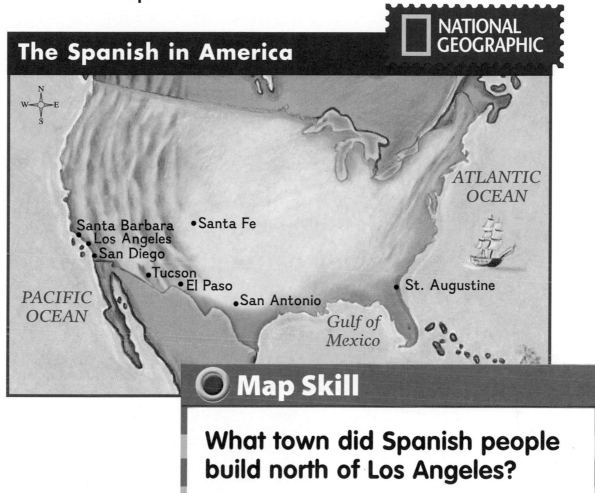

The Spanish in America

NATIONAL GEOGRAPHIC

ATLANTIC OCEAN

Santa Barbara
Los Angeles
San Diego
Santa Fe
Tucson
El Paso
San Antonio
St. Augustine

PACIFIC OCEAN

Gulf of Mexico

Map Skill

What town did Spanish people build north of Los Angeles?

Think and Write!

1. **What is a mission?**

2. **Would you like to be an explorer? Why or why not?**

The Pilgrims Arrive

Words to Know

colony
colonist

People from other countries came to America. The Pilgrims were a group of people who traveled from England to America. They sailed on a ship called the *Mayflower*. They came to America for a better life.

The *Mayflower*

The Pilgrims built a **colony** called Plymouth. A colony is a place that is ruled by another country. Plymouth was ruled by England. It later became part of the larger colony of Massachusetts.

A person who lives in a colony is called a **colonist**. The Pilgrims, or colonists, had a hard winter. In the spring they met the Native Americans who lived nearby. They helped the colonists.

What is a colony?

Living in Colonies

The Pilgrims did not know how to live in their new home. One Native American named Squanto had once lived in England. He knew how to speak English. Squanto stayed with the Pilgrims to help them. He showed them how to fish, hunt, and grow food.

The First Thanksgiving

Squanto and the Pilgrims

By fall, the Pilgrims had lots of food. They made a big meal. Squanto and the Native Americans came to the meal. The Pilgrims thanked God for their new friends and for all the good things that had happened.

 How did Squanto help the Pilgrims?

Think and Write!

1 Why did the Pilgrims come to America?

2 Why do you think the Pilgrims invited the Native Americans to their meal?

Being a Good Citizen
Keeping History Alive

Mrs. Talbert's class at J.H. Gunn School in Charlotte, North Carolina, heard some surprising news. Their old brick building would soon be torn down. A new school would be built. Kristen Hargis says, "We all felt sad. We like our school."

"We decided to make a video of our school and the people who had gone there," says Ira Grier. "My grandma went to our school just like me!"

Ira's grandma

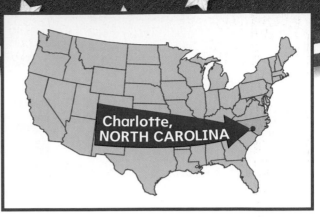

Charlotte,
NORTH CAROLINA

Ira's grandma and other students from the past visited the class. The children interviewed them while the teacher made a video. The tape will be kept in the library of the new school. That way, everyone can watch it and remember the old school.

Elva Grier

NO TRESPASSING DUE TO CONSTRUCTION

 Be a Good Citizen

What are some ways you can help remember people or places?

Activity

Find out about something that happened in your community. Make a book that can help to remember it.

141

Lesson 4

From Colonies to States

Words to Know

independence
President

Many colonists came from England to America. They lived in 13 colonies ruled by England. Find the colonies on the map.

The colonists had to follow England's laws. Some colonists thought that this was not fair.

● Map Skill

What body of water bordered the colonies?

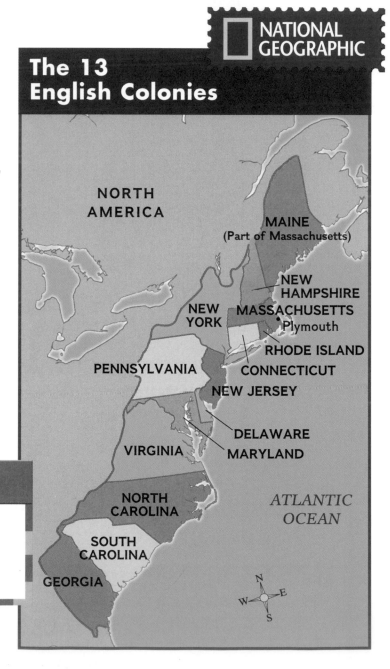

NATIONAL GEOGRAPHIC

The 13 English Colonies

NORTH AMERICA

MAINE (Part of Massachusetts)

NEW HAMPSHIRE

NEW YORK

MASSACHUSETTS
Plymouth

RHODE ISLAND

CONNECTICUT

PENNSYLVANIA

NEW JERSEY

DELAWARE

VIRGINIA

MARYLAND

NORTH CAROLINA

ATLANTIC OCEAN

SOUTH CAROLINA

GEORGIA

N
W E
S

The king of England did not want the colonies to be free. The colonies and England had a war. This war was called the American Revolution.

George Washington led the American Army against the English Army. He helped the Americans win the war.

 Why did our country fight against England?

George Washington and the American Army

Declaration of Independence

Leaders of the colonies met on July 4, 1776. They signed a paper called the Declaration of **Independence**. Independence means being free from other people or places.

The Declaration of Independence said that the 13 colonies were free from England. It said that each colony was now a state. Now all the states together were a country. It was called the United States of America.

After the war, many Americans wanted George Washington to lead our new country. George Washington became the first **President** of the United States. The President is the leader of our country.

 What happened on July 4, 1776?

The Laws of a Nation

The United States was now a free country. Americans no longer had to follow the laws of England. They needed to make their own laws.

The leaders from 12 of the 13 states had a meeting. They planned a new government. They called this plan the Constitution.

The Constitution also lists the rights of our country's citizens. One right is that we can say whatever we think without being put in jail. Another right is to be able to worship or not worship God as we wish.

 What is the Constitution?

Think and Write!

1 What did the Declaration of Independence say?

2 Why do you think people wanted George Washington to be our country's first President?

Comparing Sources

You can learn about the past from many different **sources**. A source is something that gives information. Letters, books, photographs, speeches, paintings, and interviews are all sources.

The painting below is a source of information. It shows the day that George Washington said goodbye to his officers when the war was over. You can see him hugging one of his officers. You can see sad faces. You can see three other officers crying.

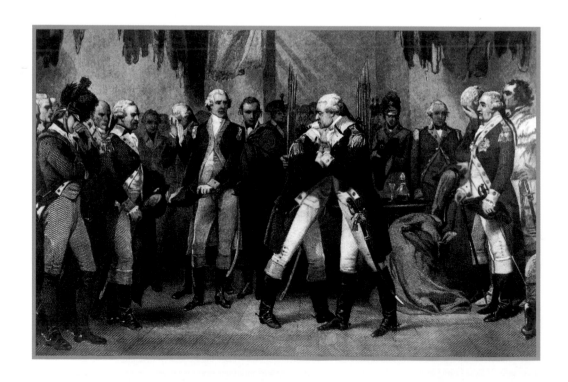

Benjamin Tallmadge was one of George Washington's officers. He wrote a book. This book is another source of information about the day that Washington said goodbye. Read what he wrote and then answer the questions.

> "Such a scene of sorrow and weeping I had never before witnessed."

Try The Skill

1. What can you tell about the day that Washington said goodbye to his officers from reading what Benjamin Tallmadge wrote?

2. Compare the two sources. How is what Benjamin Tallmadge wrote like the painting? How is it different from the painting?

 **Make It!** Think of something you and a partner did or saw together. Have one partner draw what happened, and the other write what happened. Compare them.

Celebrate History with Art

Spirit of '76

by Archibald M. Willard

This painting was first named "Yankee Doodle." It shows people marching together for freedom during the American Revolution. The painting was renamed "Spirit of '76" during a celebration for our country's 100th birthday in 1876.

Our Country at War

Our country was free from England. But not all people in our country were free. Many states had laws that allowed **slavery** . Slavery is one person owning another.

Enslaved African Americans had to work long hours without pay. They were not allowed to read or write. They were not free. Many tried to escape. Escape means to run away.

Harriet Tubman

152

Harriet Tubman escaped from slavery. Then she helped other enslaved people escape.

Frederick Douglass also escaped from slavery. He gave great speeches against slavery.

Frederick Douglass

 What is slavery?

The Civil War

Many people in the northern part of our country wanted laws against slavery. Many people in the southern part wanted to keep slavery. President Abraham Lincoln was against slavery. Read what Lincoln said about slavery.

In his own words

"If slavery is not wrong, then nothing is wrong. I cannot remember when I did not so think and feel."

—by *Abraham Lincoln*

Northern Soldier

There was a war between the states of the North and the South. It was called the Civil War. A civil war is a war that is fought between people who live in the same country.

Some people said that the war was about slavery. Others said that it was about the right of each state to choose its own way of life.

The North won the war in 1865. After the war ended, slavery was against the law.

Southern Soldier

What happened after the Civil War ended?

Think and Write!

1 What was one reason that the North and South fought the Civil War?

2 Why did many people want to escape from slavery?

Biography

Sojourner Truth

Sojourner Truth
22
Black Heritage USA

Isabella Baumfree was an enslaved person in New York. When she escaped slavery, she changed her name to Sojourner Truth.

Sojourner Truth became a famous speaker. She was the first African American woman to make speeches against slavery. She also gave speeches to say that women should have more rights.

FREE LECTURE!

SOJOURNER TRUTH,

Who has been a slave in the State of New York, and who has been a Lecturer for the last twenty-three years, whose characteristics have been so vividly portrayed by Mrs. Harriet Beecher Stowe, as the African Nybil, will deliver a lecture upon the present issues of the day,

At   On

And will give her experience as a Slave mother and religious woman. She comes highly recommended as a public speaker, having the approval of many thousands who have heard her earnest appeals, among whom are Wendell Phillips, Wm. Lloyd Garrison, and other distinguished men of the nation.

☞ At the close of her discourse she will offer for sale her photograph and a few of her choice songs.

Sojourner Truth met with President Abraham Lincoln in the White House. He asked her to stay in Washington, D.C., to help people who had been enslaved. She helped them find jobs and homes.

Explore more about the life of Sojourner Truth at our Web site www.mhschool.com

From Sea to Sea

The land in the East, along the Atlantic Ocean, was getting crowded. People began to move west toward the Pacific Ocean. These people were called **pioneers**. Pioneers are people who leave their homes to lead the way into a land that they do not know.

It was very hard for the pioneers to travel with no roads or paths. Often they had no food. Sometimes Native Americans attacked them.

Native Americans in the East had already lost most of their land. Now the Native Americans from the West were forced to leave their land or share it with the pioneers.

Why did the pioneers move west?

America Grows

Today, people still come from different countries to live in the United States. Many come here for a better life. They are called **immigrants**. An immigrant is a person who leaves one country to live in another.

Immigrants bring many traditions with them from their countries. They bring songs, art, dances, and stories. They also bring new languages and new foods.

What things do immigrants bring to our country?

Think and Write!

1. **What happened to Native Americans when pioneers moved to the West?**

2. **Why do immigrants still come to the United States?**

Using Time Lines

A **time line** is a line that shows the order in which things happen.

This time line shows some things that happened in America's history between 1492 and 2001.

The first box shows that Columbus sailed to North America in 1492.

Four Dates in American History

1492

Columbus sails to North America.

The Declaration of Independence is signed.

Try The Skill

1. What happened in 2001?

2. In what year did slavery end?

 Make your own time line about the history of your community in the past three years.

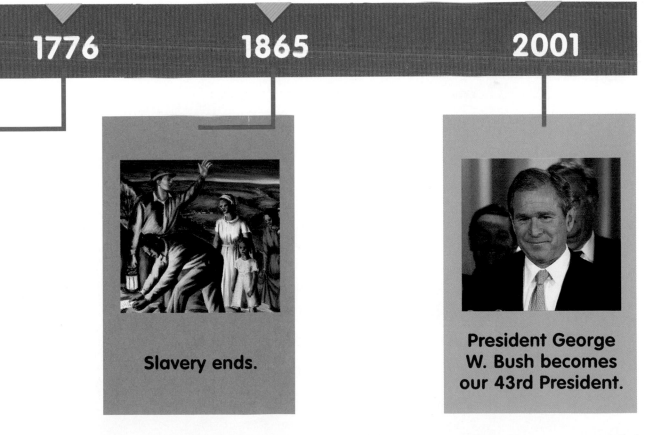

| 1776 | 1865 | 2001 |

Slavery ends.

President George W. Bush becomes our 43rd President.

A Community's History

Many communities keep stories of their past alive. In this lesson, you will read about the history of Dayton, Ohio.

The Adena were a group of Native Americans who lived in Ohio in **ancient times**. Ancient times are times that happened very long ago.

Miamisburg Mound

The place in Ohio where the Adena lived had three rivers. They used the rivers for water and travel. They used arrowheads for hunting.

The Adena built a mound, or pile of earth, called the Miamisburg Mound. They buried their dead with jewelry and other items in the mound.

What are ancient times?

arrowhead

The City of Dayton, Ohio

In **modern times**, some people from the city of Cincinnati, Ohio, looked for a new place to live. Modern times are times that are happening now, or times that happened a short while ago.

The people from Cincinnati found the same land where the Adena had lived. They liked the land and the three rivers near the land. The three rivers could be used for water and travel. They named the area Dayton.

NATIONAL GEOGRAPHIC

The Three Rivers of Dayton

Stilwater River

Great Miami River

Mad River

N
W   E
S

◉ Map Skill

What three rivers are in Dayton?

Dayton was also home to Wilbur and Orville Wright. They were brothers who invented the first airplane.

The Wright Brothers

Today Dayton is a busy city. But it still keeps its history alive. You can visit the Miamisburg Mound. You can watch the same three rivers flow that were used by the Adena. You can visit the place where the Wright Brothers worked.

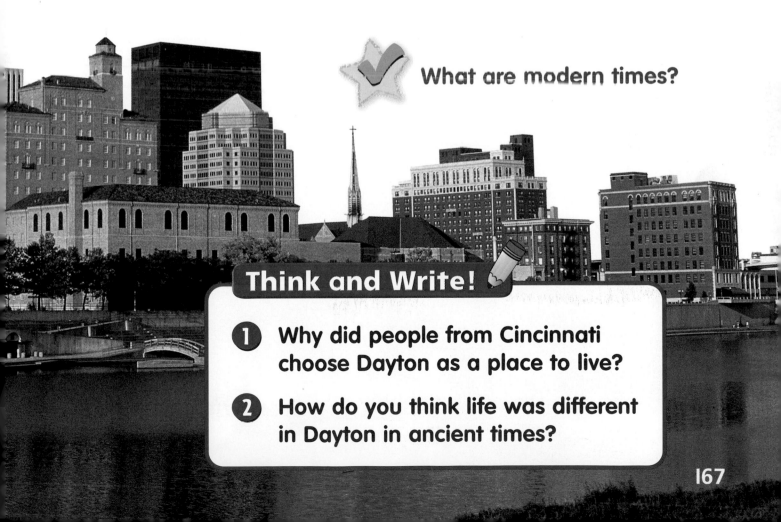

What are modern times?

Think and Write!

1 Why did people from Cincinnati choose Dayton as a place to live?

2 How do you think life was different in Dayton in ancient times?

A Look at Australia's First People

Aboriginal people were the first people to have lived on the continent of Australia. The word "aboriginal" means *first*.

Aboriginal people of Australia lived there in ancient times. They live there in modern times, too!

Today, Australia's Aboriginal people follow many of their old traditions.

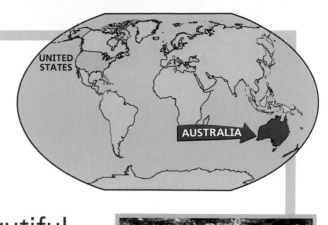

Long ago, they painted beautiful drawings on bark and rocks. Today many modern Aboriginal artists paint the same way as they did long ago.

Aboriginal rock art

Aboriginal painting

Talk about it!

What tradition is followed by Aboriginal people today?

169

Words to Know

Choose the word or words that best tell about each sentence.

history explorer Native Americans

1. This is a person who travels to a new place to learn about it.

2. This is the story of the past.

3. These were the first people to live in America.

Check Your Reading

4. What kind of problems did the pioneers face as they moved west?

5. Why did the leaders of the thirteen colonies sign the Constitution?

6. How are ancient times and modern times different?

Compare Sources

Look at the photograph. It shows immigrants on a ship coming to America. They are arriving in New York harbor.

Elizabeth Phillips was an immigrant who came to America on a ship. She also arrived in New York harbor. She was interviewed about her trip. Read what she said and then answer the questions.

"The first time I saw the Statue of Liberty all the people were rushing to the side of the boat. 'Look at her, look at her.'"

7. What can you tell by looking at the photograph and reading the interview?

8. Compare the two sources. How are the photograph and the interview alike? How are they different?

Use a Time Line

9. In what season and year did the Pilgrims come to America?

The Pilgrim's Year		
Winter, 1620	**Spring, 1621**	**Fall, 1621**

The Pilgrims come to America.	The Pilgrims meet Native Americans.	The Pilgrims have a big feast.

Sort Into Groups

TEST PREP

10. Which picture does not go with  ?

◯   ◯   ◯

Activity

Write a Song

* Write words about people or places from history.

* Think of a tune you know.

* Put the words to the tune.

* Share your song with your class.

Our country wasn't free,
We wanted liberty,
Great heroes like George Washington
Fought hard for victory!

Think and Write

What person from history would you like to meet? Write about that person.

For more information about this unit, visit our Web site at **www.mhschool.com**

173

Literature

Our Car Wash

by Lily Close

illustrated by Jean Hirashima

Come to our car wash.
We'll work hard for you.
We wash big and small cars
And cars that are blue!

We wash bikes and trucks.
We huff and we puff!
We work and we work
'Til enough is *enough!*

CAR
WASH
$1.50

175

We have so much money
From our work today.
Now we can buy lots
Of fun games to play!

176

Or maybe we'll save it.
Yes! That's what we'll do.
Then someday we'll buy
Our own car that's blue!

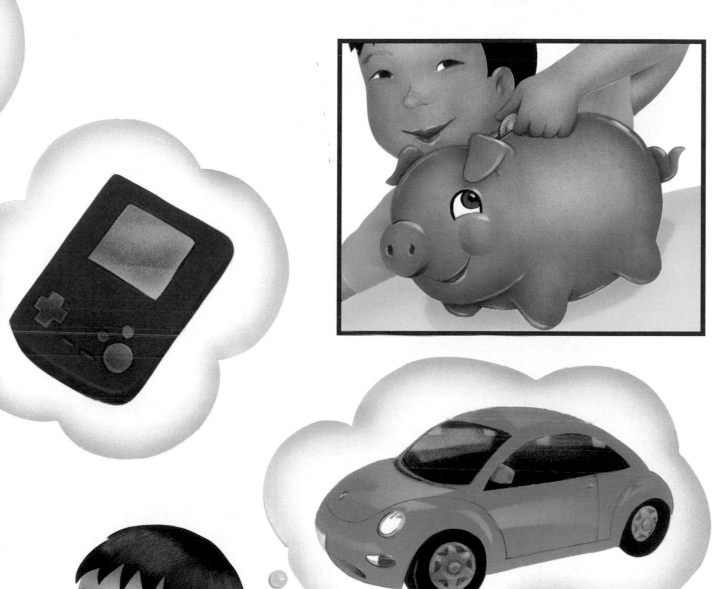

Talk about it!

**What work could you do
to make money?**

177

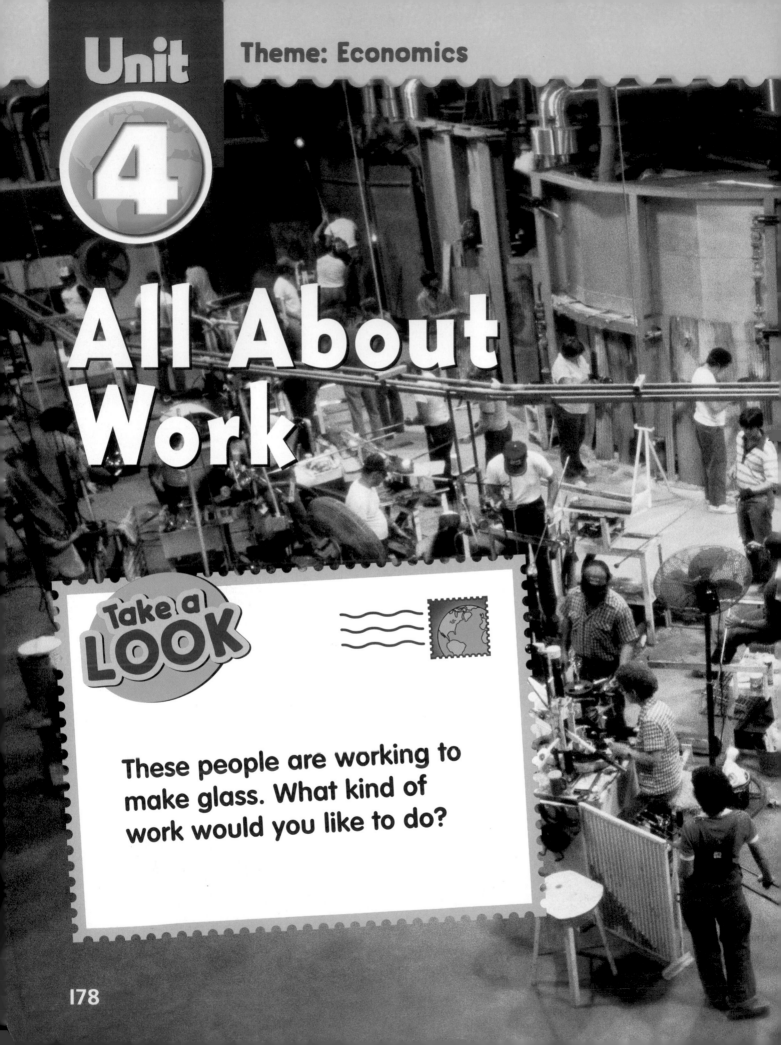

Unit 4

All About Work

Take a LOOK

These people are working to make glass. What kind of work would you like to do?

Explore work at our Web site **www.mhschool.com**

179

The Big Idea

Why Do People Work?

People work for many reasons. Read what Rita says about why people work.

"I rake leaves to make money to buy a game."

"My mom works to pay for our food and clothes."

"My neighbor works as a police officer. He makes money by keeping people safe."

In the United States people are free to choose the work they do. In this unit you will learn about the different jobs people do.

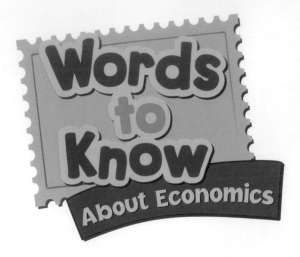

Words to Know

About Economics

Find the pictures and say the words.

volunteer

goods

consumer

factory

Talk about it!

What is happening in this picture?

Lesson 1

Many Jobs

Words to Know

earn
tax
volunteer

Many people have jobs. Most people work at a job to **earn** money. Earn means to get paid money for work you do.

People work in many different places. Some people go to an office. Some people work in a store.

184

Not all people work in offices and stores. Some people do their jobs at home. Others travel to do their work. Some people work outdoors.

Why do most people work?

Community Jobs

There are special jobs that help everyone in a community. Police officers, teachers, bus drivers, and firefighters help the whole community. Everyone in the community shares in paying for these jobs.

Look at the pictures on these pages. First, each person pays a **tax**. A tax is money that people pay to a community. Next, the community collects all of the tax money. Finally, the community pays the workers for the work they do.

Why do people in a community pay tax money?

Volunteers

A person who works but is not paid is called a **volunteer**. Volunteers do many important jobs.

Some volunteers work in schools or hospitals. Other volunteers bring food to people who cannot leave their homes.

Volunteers also help when people are in trouble because of floods or earthquakes. Without volunteers, many important jobs would not get done.

Some volunteers travel to help people in other communities or countries. One such volunteer is former U.S. President Jimmy Carter. He and other volunteers build houses for people who need them. Read what Jimmy Carter wrote about being a volunteer.

In his own words

"It's fulfilling; it's a wonderful experience for us."
— Jimmy Carter

What are some jobs that volunteers do?

Working at Home

Today, many people choose to work from home. More people than ever have computers. These people can do office work without ever leaving home!

Sometimes, one parent works at home by taking care of the house and family. Often the other parent works outside the home to earn money.

Doctors and lawyers can work from home, too. They set up offices in their homes.

Some carpenters, artists, and other people with special skills, also work at home. Sometimes, they turn part of their homes into a workshop or a store.

 What kinds of work can people do at home?

Think and Write!

1 **Name some jobs people do that help the whole community.**

2 **What kind of volunteer work would you like to do?**

CITIZENSHIP

Being a Good Citizen
The Hat Factory

Mrs. Palmer's students in McGaheysville, Virginia, started a business called Hats R Us. They made 120 hats out of soft cloth. Some students cut the cloth. Others pinned it or helped sew it. "Three moms came with their sewing machines," says Joaquin Gonzalez. "They helped too."

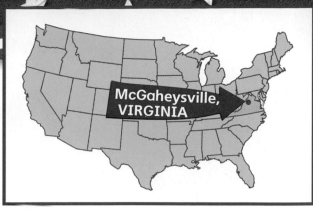

McGaheysville, VIRGINIA

The children sold all the hats in three days and made $950. They used some of the money to take a bus trip to Richmond, the state capital of Virginia. They used the rest of the money to buy more cloth and make more hats!

Then, they traveled to a hospital and gave the new hats to sick children. Joaquin said, "I learned about working. I am proud of what we did."

Joaquin Gonzalez

⭐ Be a Good Citizen

What do you like about working?

Activity

Think of different ways you can earn money. Share your ideas with friends and start a business.

Our Needs and Wants

There are certain things that people must have to live. These things are called **needs**. Every person needs food, clothing, love, and **shelter**. Shelter is a place where people live. The pictures on this page show needs.

194

The pictures on this page show **wants**. Wants are things people would like to have but do not need in order to live.

People cannot buy everything that they want. Often they have to make a choice. Which of the wants on this page would you choose?

Think and Write!

1. What do people need in order to live?

2. What is the difference between needs and wants?

Goods and Services

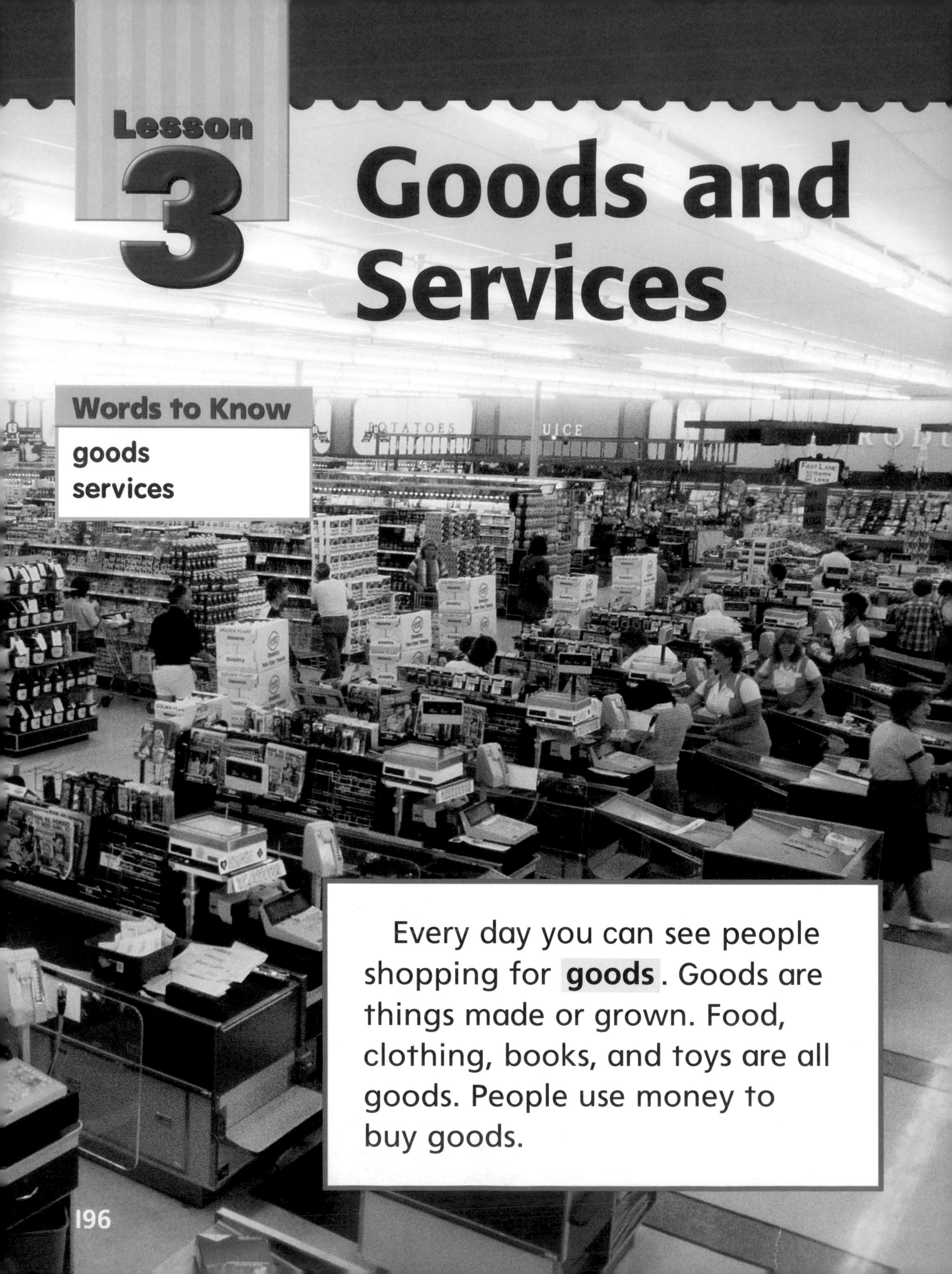

Words to Know

goods
services

Every day you can see people shopping for **goods**. Goods are things made or grown. Food, clothing, books, and toys are all goods. People use money to buy goods.

People also use money to buy **services**. A service is something useful that people do for others.

There are many different kinds of service work. Doctors, barbers, and taxi drivers are all service workers. These workers get paid for the services they do. What service work do you see in your community?

 What is a service?

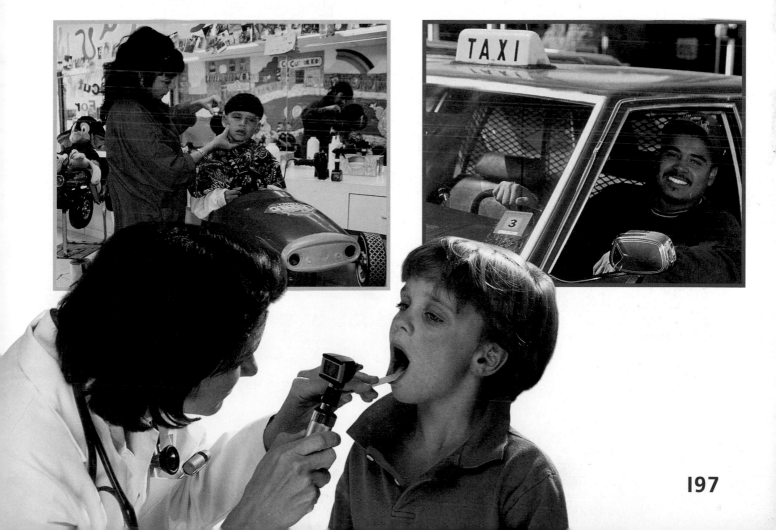

A Savings Plan

Every time you pay for goods or services, you are spending money. Spending means that you pay money for something.

If you spend all of your money at once, you will not have any left over. That's why many people save their money. Save means to keep your money to use later.

To save money, you can make a savings plan. For example, each time you earn money, you can put some of it in a bank. Soon you will have enough saved to buy something you want.

$5.00

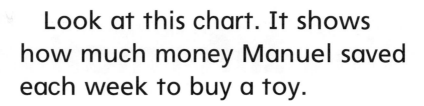

Look at this chart. It shows how much money Manuel saved each week to buy a toy.

Using Charts

Manuel's Savings	
Week 1	$ .50
Week 2	$1.50
Week 3	$2.00
Week 4	$1.00
Total	$5.00

Chart Skill

How much money did Manuel save altogether by week 3?

Think and Write!

1 Why is it important for people to save money?

2 What goods and services does your family buy?

Locating Information

You can locate, or find, information in books and computers.

The **table of contents** is in the front of a book. It tells you the name of each lesson or chapter in the book. It also tells you on what pages they are located. Look at the table of contents from a book about work. It shows that Chapter 3 is called "Work You Can Do at Home." It begins on page 27.

Table of Contents

Index

The **index** is in the back of a book. It tells you the name and page number of people, places, and things in the book. Look at the index. It shows that information about service can be found on page 84.

You can also use a computer to find information. A **keyword** is the main word you type when you search for a topic on the Internet. The keyword for this search is "jobs."

Try The Skill

1. What chapter tells about service jobs?

2. Which pages tell you about saving money?

 **Make a list of keywords to find information about different kinds of shelter.**

Producers and Consumers

This farmer grows apples to sell. She is a **producer**. A producer makes or grows goods to sell.

This potter is also a producer. He is making pottery to sell.

The farmer and potter will sell their goods to a store or market. Then people will come to the store or market to buy the goods.

A **consumer** uses the goods made by a producer. Consumers eat or use things that are grown or made by a producer.

When is a person a producer?

203

We Are All Consumers

Everyone is a consumer. That is because we all have needs and wants.

When the farmer grows apples to sell, she is a producer. But when the farmer buys a piece of pottery that she wants, she is a consumer!

When the potter makes things for people to buy, he is a producer. But when he buys and eats food that he needs, he is a consumer!

 Why are we all consumers?

Think and Write!

1. What is the difference between a producer and a consumer?

2. What would happen if we did not have enough producers?

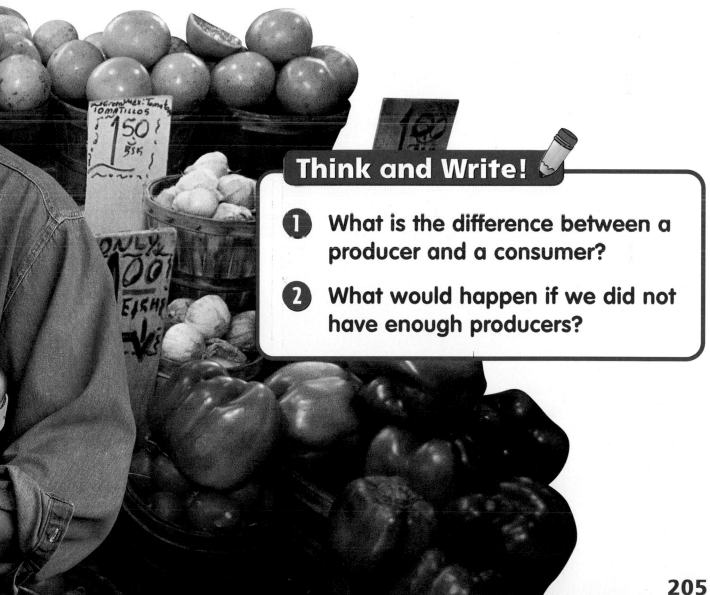

Celebrate Work
with a Poem

This poem is about farmworkers. Farmworkers work long and hard picking fruits and vegetables for us to eat.

Farmworkers

by Alma Flor Ada

Farmworkers is the name we give
to the people who work the
land, who harvest the fields,
united beneath one sky.

Thank you, farmworker,
for the fruits your hands have brought me.
I will grow stronger and kinder
as I eat what you have grown.

From Farm to Factory

Words to Know

factory

Trees are a natural resource. Trees are used to make many things like paper, chairs, and paper towels.

Have you ever wondered how paper towels are made? In this lesson, you will find out!

First, the trees are planted in a tree farm. They are watered to help them grow.

When the trees are fully grown, they are cut down.

Douglas Fir

208

Then, the trees are taken to a paper **factory**. A factory is a building where things are made.

What happens to the trees when they are grown?

At the Paper Factory

At the paper factory, the trees will be made into paper towels. A paper factory is also called a pulp mill.

First, the trees are chopped into small chips of wood. Other things are mixed in with the chips.

Then, they are heated. This makes the chips very soft. These soft wood chips are called pulp. Bleach is added to make the color of the pulp turn from brown to white.

Next, the pulp is dried and pressed into long sheets. Then, the sheets are rolled and cut.

The paper towels are ready to be packaged and sent to stores for consumers to buy.

 What happens to the trees when they reach the pulp mill or paper factory?

Think and Write!

1 What causes the brown pulp to turn white?

2 What are all the steps to make paper towels from trees?

Following Routes on a Map

A **route** is a way of going from one place to another. You can follow a route on a map.

Find the Red Apple Farm truck on Roberts Drive. The driver is bringing apples to the Farmer's Market to sell to the consumers. Suppose that the driver turned right at Lark Lane. Find Lark Lane with your finger.

Truck Route

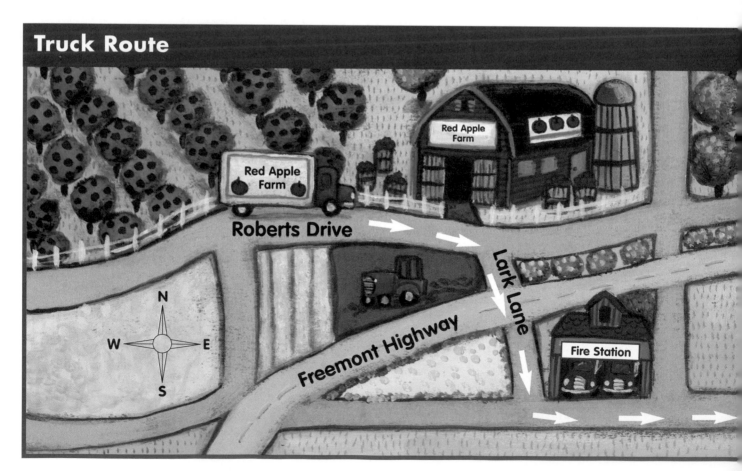

SKILLS

Try The Skill

1. What highway will the driver pass on Lark Lane?

2. On what street should the driver turn to get to the Farmer's Market?

 Make your own map. Show a route a truck might follow to a store in your neighborhood.

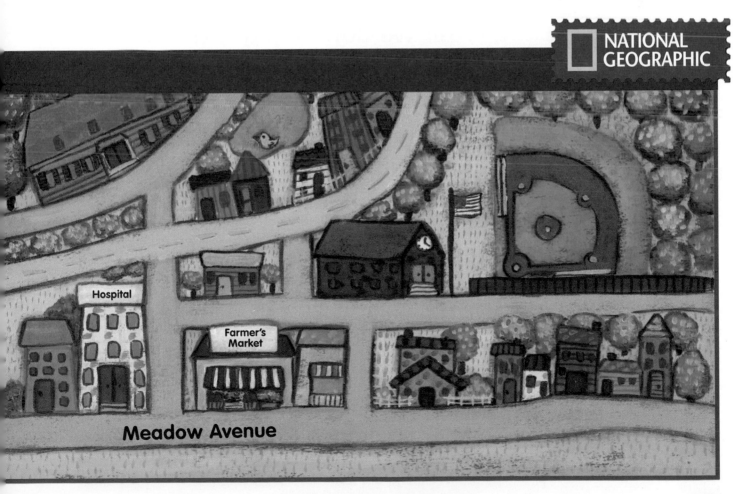

Trading with Other Countries

In the United States, we have lots of farmland. Almost half of the world's corn is grown here!

But we don't need that much corn. So we **trade** with other countries. Trade means to give something and then get something back. When countries trade, they buy and sell goods and services.

For example, Japan does not have enough farmland to grow corn. We trade with Japan by selling them corn. In return, Japan sells televisions and cars to us.

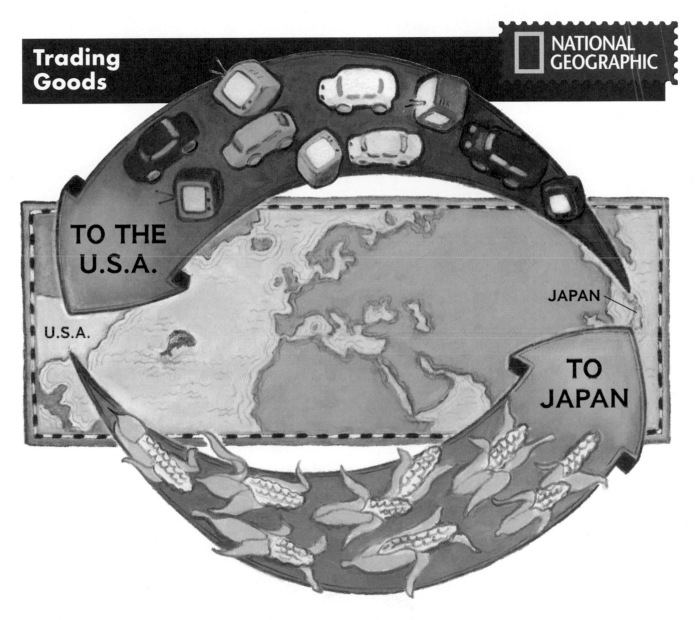

Trading Goods

NATIONAL GEOGRAPHIC

TO THE U.S.A.

U.S.A.

JAPAN

TO JAPAN

 Why do countries trade?

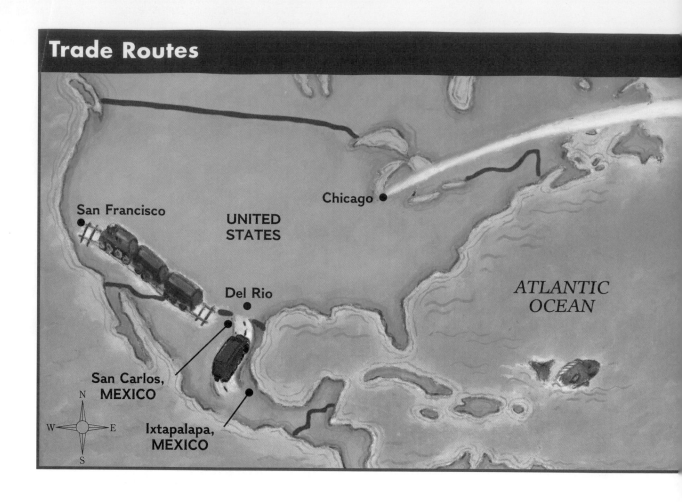

Trade Routes

San Francisco

UNITED STATES

Chicago

Del Rio

San Carlos, MEXICO

Ixtapalapa, MEXICO

ATLANTIC OCEAN

N
W E
S

Trading Routes

Many kinds of transportation are used to carry goods for trading. Countries close to each other use trucks or trains. Countries far apart use airplanes or ships. The route, or way goods travel from one place to another, is called a trade route.

Mexico is very close to the United States. The goods we trade are sent in trains or trucks. The map above shows trade routes between the United States and Mexico.

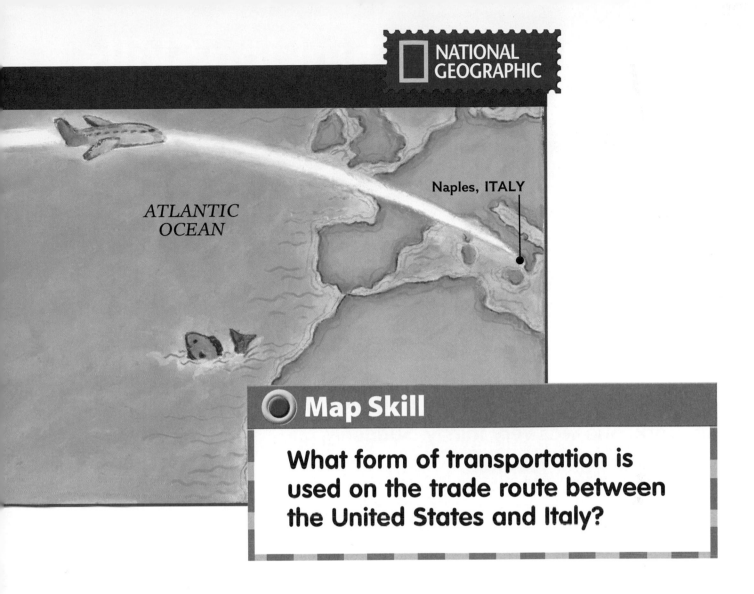

ATLANTIC
OCEAN

Naples, ITALY

Map Skill

What form of transportation is used on the trade route between the United States and Italy?

The map also shows a trade route between the United States and Italy.

The United States and Italy are far apart. Airplanes fly across the ocean to carry the goods we trade back and forth.

Think and Write!

1 What is a trade route?

2 What might happen if countries did not trade?

Making Predictions

A **prediction** is a guess about what will happen next. First, you need to find out what has already happened. Then, you can guess what might happen next.

Read this paragraph:

The sun was very hot. Eve raced through the park. She was very thirsty. Suddenly, she saw a water fountain.

What do you think might happen next? Did you make a prediction that Eve will get a drink at the fountain?

Read this paragraph and then answer the questions.

There are two islands. The people on the first island make only peanut butter. The people on the second island make only grape jelly. They are tired of eating only one kind of food. There is a boat that can travel from one island to the other.

Try The Skill

1. What has happened so far?

2. What will probably happen next?
   Why do you think so?

 Draw a picture. Tell what has happened so far, and what might happen next.

New Ways to Meet Needs

We will always have needs and wants. But the *way* our needs and wants are met changes over time.

Technology is using science to make things faster, easier, or better. New technology changes the way our needs and wants are met.

stone wheel

Long ago, farmers planted seeds and picked fruits and vegetables by hand. New technology has made it possible for farmers to do this work with machines.

Long ago, it took weeks to travel by horse and wagon. New technology has made it possible for people to travel quickly by train, car, or plane. The pictures below show how new technology made transportation better after the wheel was invented.

 What kinds of new technology does your family use at home?

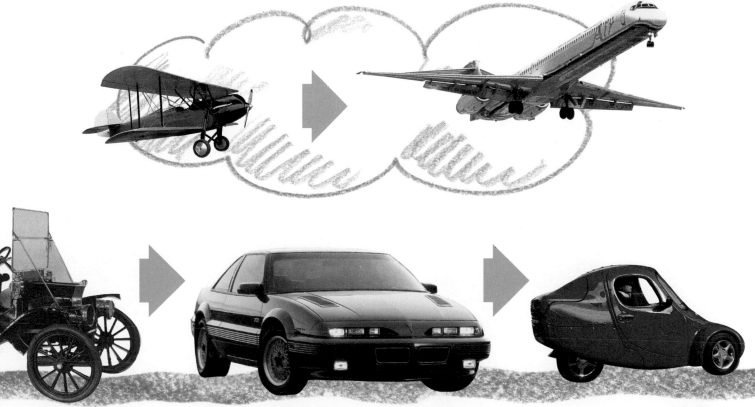

Helios Aircraft

Today and Tomorrow

New technology changes the way people work and live. More than ever, people use new technology in their jobs.

Computers have many new uses. Computers in tiny cameras and robots help doctors do surgery. Music groups use computers to make music and videos.

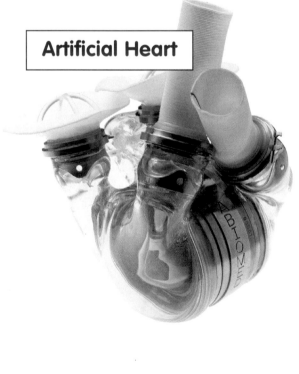

Artificial Heart

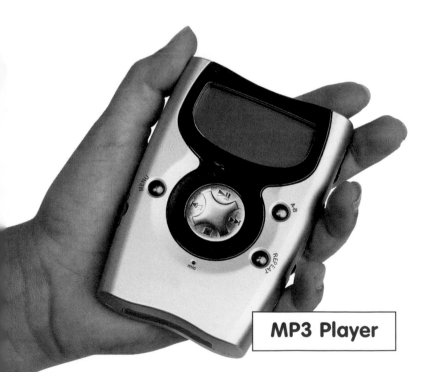

MP3 Player

New technology is changing the way our needs and wants are met every day. No one knows for sure what our future will be. Our dreams today may be what is real tomorrow!

What kinds of things do you think you will do in the future?

Think and Write!

1 What are some new uses for computers?

2 How does new technology help you at school?

Biography

Robert Fulton

Robert Fulton was a great inventor. An inventor is a person who makes something that has never been made before. As a boy, Robert loved to draw and make things. He even made his own pencils!

The Clermont

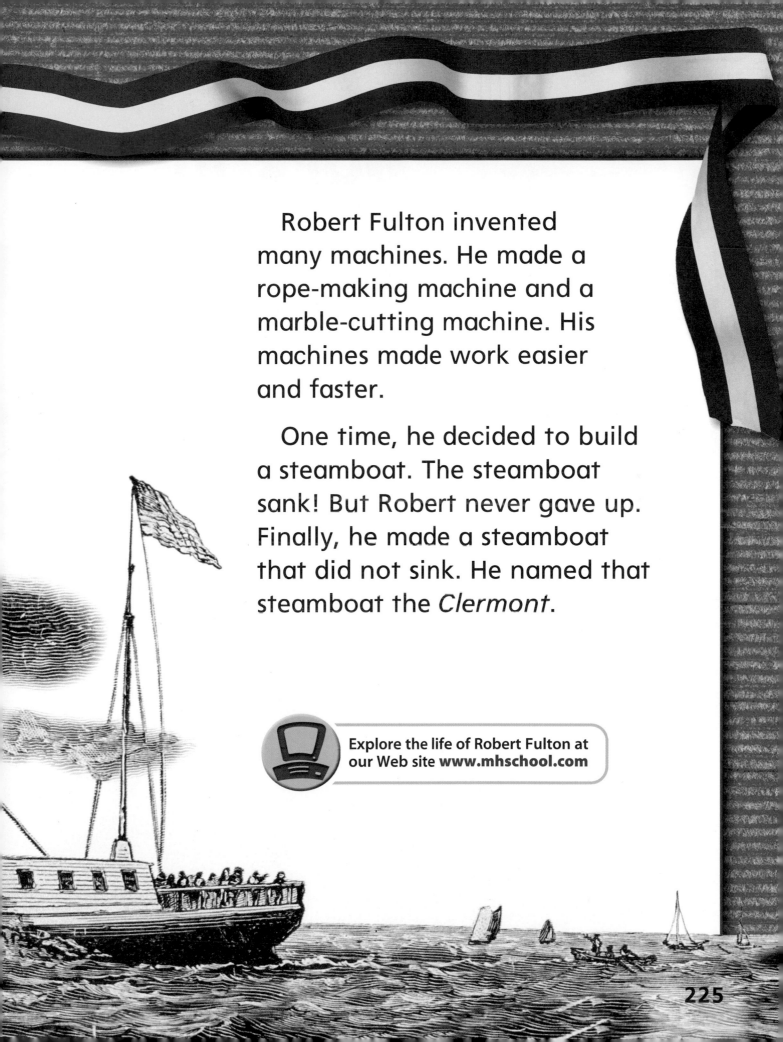

Robert Fulton invented many machines. He made a rope-making machine and a marble-cutting machine. His machines made work easier and faster.

One time, he decided to build a steamboat. The steamboat sank! But Robert never gave up. Finally, he made a steamboat that did not sink. He named that steamboat the *Clermont*.

Explore the life of Robert Fulton at our Web site **www.mhschool.com**

A Look at Work in China

People in China work at many different jobs. Some people do service work as doctors, teachers, and police officers. Others are farmers who grow lots of cotton and rice.

In China, most people ride bicycles to work. China is often called "the land of the bicycle." That is because China makes more than 30 million bicycles each year. They have special parking lots just for bicycles!

UNITED STATES

CHINA

Talk about it!

Why is China called "the land of the bicycle"?

Words to Know

volunteer	consumer	goods

1. A ____ is someone who uses the goods made by a producer.

2. ____ are things that people make or grow.

3. When you don't get paid for doing work, you are a ____.

Check Your Reading

4. Why do some workers get paid with tax money?

5. How does new technology help us?

6. Name some kinds of service workers.

Locate Information

Look at the table of contents below and then answer the questions.

Table of Contents

7. On which page can you begin reading about the *Clermont*?

8. What chapter would you read to learn more about Fulton's rope-making machine?

 Make a picture book about jobs. Then make a table of contents for your book.

● Follow Routes on a Map

Use the map below to answer the question about the train route.

Train Route

NATIONAL GEOGRAPHIC

Oakville

Seatown

9. Which town will the train pass on its way to Oakville?

● Make Predictions

TEST PREP

Read the paragraph below. Then answer the question.

> Joe drove his car down the street. Suddenly, his tire got flat. He saw a sign across the street that read, "Tires for Sale."

10. What will Joe probably do next?

   read a book   eat lunch   buy a tire

   ⬭   ⬭   ⬭

Activity

"All Kinds of Work" Collage

* Gather scissors, magazines, glue, markers, and a large sheet of paper.

* Cut out pictures of people working from magazines.

* Glue the pictures onto a large sheet of paper.

* Label each picture with the name of the job the worker does.

Think and Write

How do you think trade helps countries to get along?

For more information about this unit, visit our Web site at **www.mhschool.com**

Literature

Let's Choose a Name!

by Matthew Evans

illustrated by Michelle Noiset

Mrs. Lopez brought her new puppy to class. "It's your job to help choose a name!" she told the boys and girls.

Alan said, "Let's name him *Squeakers* because he likes to squeak his new toy!"

Ana said, "Let's name him *Bootsie* because it looks like he's wearing white boots!"

Jimmy said, "Let's name him *Wags* because he keeps wagging his tail!"

Mrs. Lopez said, "I like all of these names. But we can only choose one. Write down the name that you like the best."

"Wait, Mrs. Lopez," said Cami. "I think the puppy keeps trying to tell us something. Maybe he wants to be called *Spot*!"

Mrs. Lopez smiled and added the name *Spot* to the list. Then the children wrote down their choices.

"Most of you chose *Spot*," said Mrs. Lopez. "So *Spot* it is! I think *Spot* likes his name, too!"

Talk about it!

What is something that your class could choose to do?

235

Unit 5

Our Government

Take a Look

These people worked to solve problems in our country long ago. Do you know how we solve problems in our country today?

The Signing of the Constitution

Explore our government at our Web site **www.mhschool.com**

The Big Idea

How Does Our Government Work?

A **government** is the group of people who run a community, state, or country. Read what Lisa has learned about how our government works.

"The center of our country's government is located in Washington, D.C."

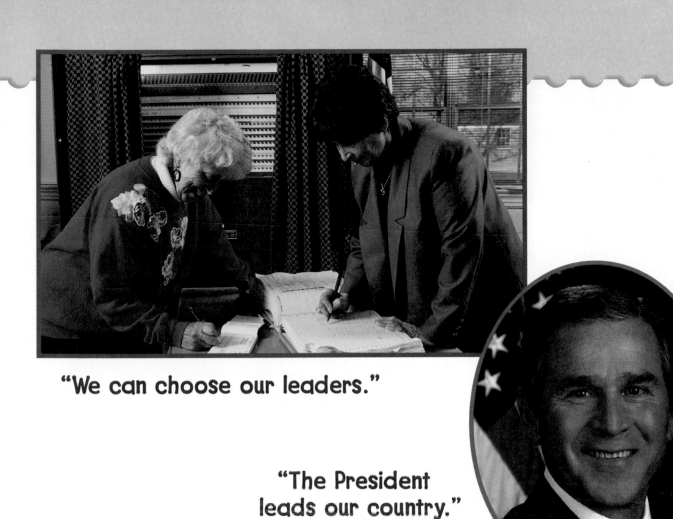

"We can choose our leaders."

"The President
leads our country."

"We believe that all people
should be treated equally."

Americans work
together to run our
government. In this
unit you will learn
more about our
government.

239

Words to Know
About Government

Find the pictures and say the words.

court

monument

Capitol

White House

Washington, D.C.

Talk about it!

What do you see in this picture?

Lesson 1

Our Country's Government

Words to Know

mayor
governor
election
court

In our country, we follow laws from three different places. We follow laws from our community, our state, and our country. Each of these places has a leader who makes sure we follow the laws.

○ Using Charts

Our Leaders

Community	State
mayor  Wellington E. Webbs is the mayor of Denver, Colorado.	**governor**  Ruth Ann Minner is the governor of Delaware.

Wellington E. Webbs is the mayor of Denver, Colorado.

Ruth Ann Minner is the governor of Delaware.

In a community, the mayor is the leader. The **mayor** makes sure that people living in a community follow its laws.

In a state, the **governor** is the leader. The governor makes sure that all the people in a state follow that state's laws.

Our country is led by the President. The President's job is to make sure that everyone in our country follows our country's laws.

 What do leaders in our country do?

Country

President

George W. Bush is the President of the United States.

 **Chart Skill**

Who are our government's leaders?

Choosing Our Leaders

We vote for our government leaders, like the President. To vote means to choose who we are for or against. The special time when we vote for our leaders is called an **election** . In an election, the person with the most votes wins.

Two kinds of voting machines

Some government leaders are not elected. Instead, they are appointed. To appoint means to pick someone for a job. Usually these people are appointed by an elected leader. Often the mayor, governor, or President appoints people.

Supreme Court Justice Earl Warren was appointed by President Eisenhower.

President Bush appointed Christie Whitman to protect our environment.

 What is the difference between being appointed and being elected?

A Look at Community Government

Governments are made up of many people with different jobs. Let's look at a community government in a city to learn about these jobs.

Some people make laws. A group of people called the city council makes laws for a city. The mayor makes sure that people follow the city's laws.

The mayor makes sure that people follow the laws.

The city council makes the laws.

The three parts of city government

Judges make decisions about laws. A judge makes sure that laws are fair. Judges work in a **court**. People go to a court to get help when they cannot agree about the law.

 Who makes laws for a city?

A judge decides what the laws mean.

Think and Write!

1 What does the city council do?

2 How is a governor different from a mayor? How are they the same?

Biography
Thurgood Marshall

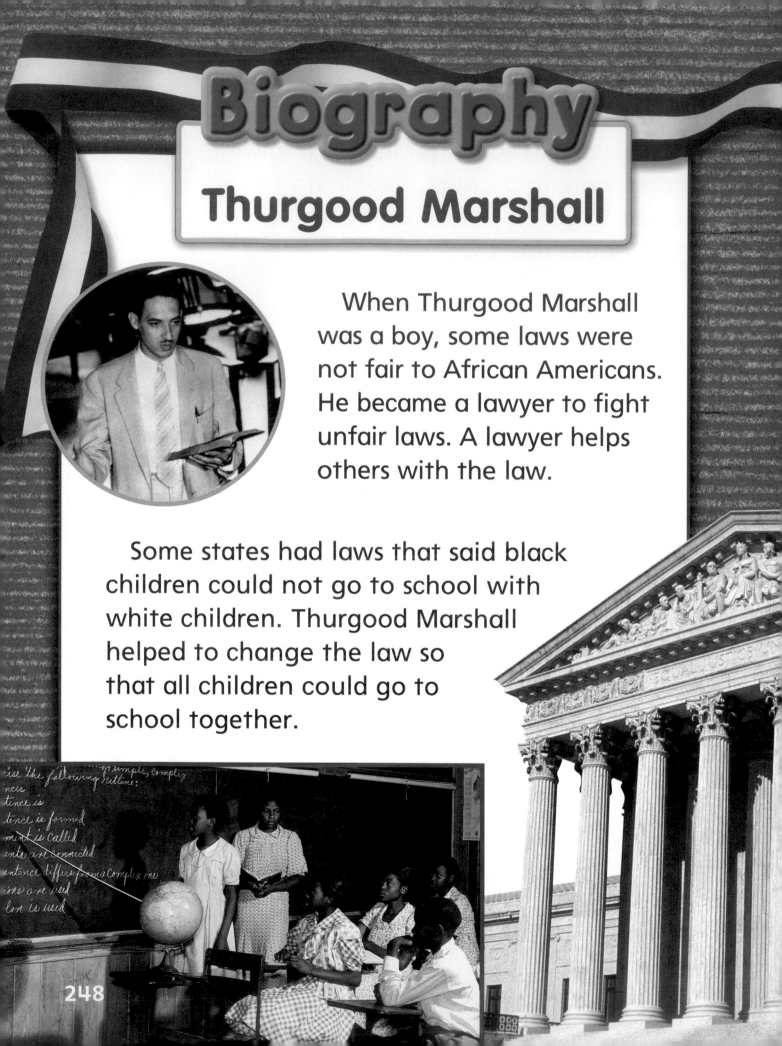

When Thurgood Marshall was a boy, some laws were not fair to African Americans. He became a lawyer to fight unfair laws. A lawyer helps others with the law.

Some states had laws that said black children could not go to school with white children. Thurgood Marshall helped to change the law so that all children could go to school together.

Thurgood Marshall was appointed by President Lyndon Johnson to be a judge on the Supreme Court. The Supreme Court is our country's most important court. Thurgood Marshall was the first African American to serve on this court. There he helped to change unfair laws for all people.

The Supreme Court in 1982

Thurgood Marshall

Explore the life of Thurgood Marshall at our Web site www.mhschool.com

Making Decisions

Choosing What Is Fair

Thurgood Marshall was a judge. He had to decide what was fair. Look at these stories. What do you think is fair?

"There is only one orange."

"We are both hungry."

"It's my turn now."

"I was here first."

★ Be a Good Citizen

Why is it important to be fair? Ask your parents, teacher, or other adult.

Activity

Act out a time when you were fair. Ask others to be in your skit.

Solving Community Problems

Communities have many needs. Tax money is used to pay for some of these needs. For example, students do not have to pay to go to public schools. Public means that something can be used by all people. This public park in Harlem, New York, is there for all people to use.

Tax money pays for public libraries, too. At a public library people can borrow books for free.

Some tax money is used to pay for public transportation, like buses and trains. Riders pay only a small amount to help cover the costs.

 Why do communities need tax money?

A Community Problem

Citizens in a community can ask to have tax money spent on community needs.

People in Harlem, New York, had a problem in their community. Workers in Harlem took down bus shelters to fix the street. But the shelters were not put back. People got wet and cold waiting for the bus in the rain and snow.

Some people who live in Harlem belong to a community board. A community board is a group of people who work to get things done to help the whole community.

Members of the community board had a meeting. They decided to meet with people who could fix the bus shelters.

 What is a community board?

Solving the Problem

Members of the community board asked New York City transportation workers to come to a meeting. The transportation workers listened to members of the community board. They agreed that bus shelters needed to be put up. Tax money was used to get the job done.

MN01304

BUS
STOP
NO
STANDING

256

Stanley Gleaton is chairman of the community board in Harlem. He says, "Your community board is here to help you with any problems you find. You and your parents can always call if you need help. The community board is here for you!"

 How were the new bus shelters paid for?

Think and Write!

1. **What problem did the citizens of Harlem solve?**

2. **What problem would you like to solve in your community?**

Using Flow Charts

A **flow chart** is a kind of chart. It shows the order in which things happen, or flow.

This flow chart shows how the citizens in Harlem got new bus shelters. To read the chart, look at number 1. It shows members of the community board talking about the problem. What is the next step?

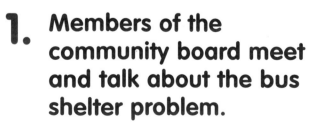

1. Members of the community board meet and talk about the bus shelter problem.

2. Members of the community board meet with New York City transportation workers.

Try The Skill

1. What happened after members of the community board talked to the transportation workers?

2. What is the last step in the flow chart?

 Make your own flow chart to show how you solved a problem.

3. New York City transportation workers have new bus shelters built.

4. Citizens use the new bus shelters.

Our Country's Capital

Words to Know

monument
Capitol
White House

The city of Washington, D.C., is the capital of the United States. This capital city is not in any state. It is a city that belongs to all of America.

Washington, D.C., has many museums and **monuments**. A monument is a building or statue that shows special respect for a person or an event.

The Washington Monument

The Capitol

The **Capitol** in Washington, D.C., is the name of a building. It is where people who work for Congress meet. Congress is the part of our government that makes laws for our country.

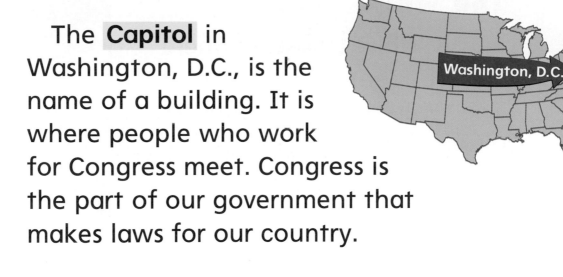

Washington, D.C.

What is our country's capital?

The Lincoln Memorial

261

The White House

The **White House** is where the President lives and works. The White House belongs to all Americans.

Many people visit the White House every year. Here are some of the rooms that visitors can see in the White House.

 Which room do you like best? Why?

The Oval Office is where the President works.

The Library has many books and important papers.

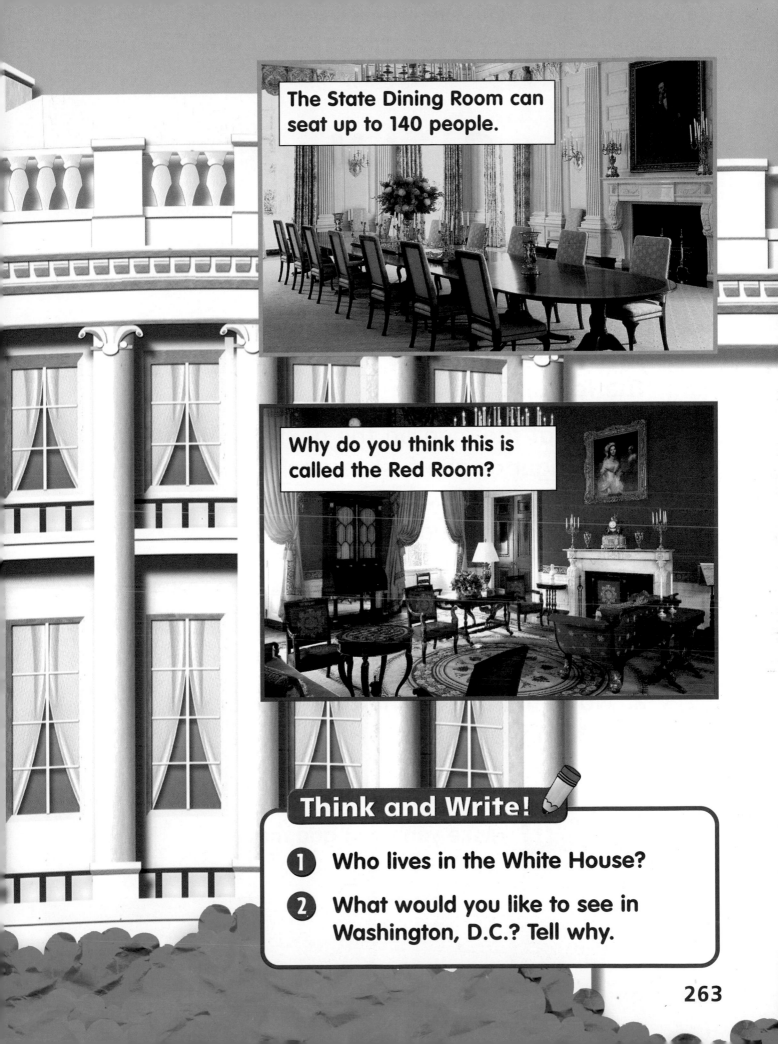

The State Dining Room can seat up to 140 people.

Why do you think this is called the Red Room?

Think and Write!

1. Who lives in the White House?

2. What would you like to see in Washington, D.C.? Tell why.

263

Using Grid Maps

A **grid map** is a map divided by lines. The lines form squares. A letter and a number name each square.

The letters are on the left and right sides of the map. The numbers are on the top and bottom.

Look at the map on the next page. Put your finger on the first square in the top row. The square is A1. Now move your finger over to square A3.

Try The Skill

1. What building is in A3?

2. Now find the Washington Monument. Which square is it in?

 **Make your own grid map.**

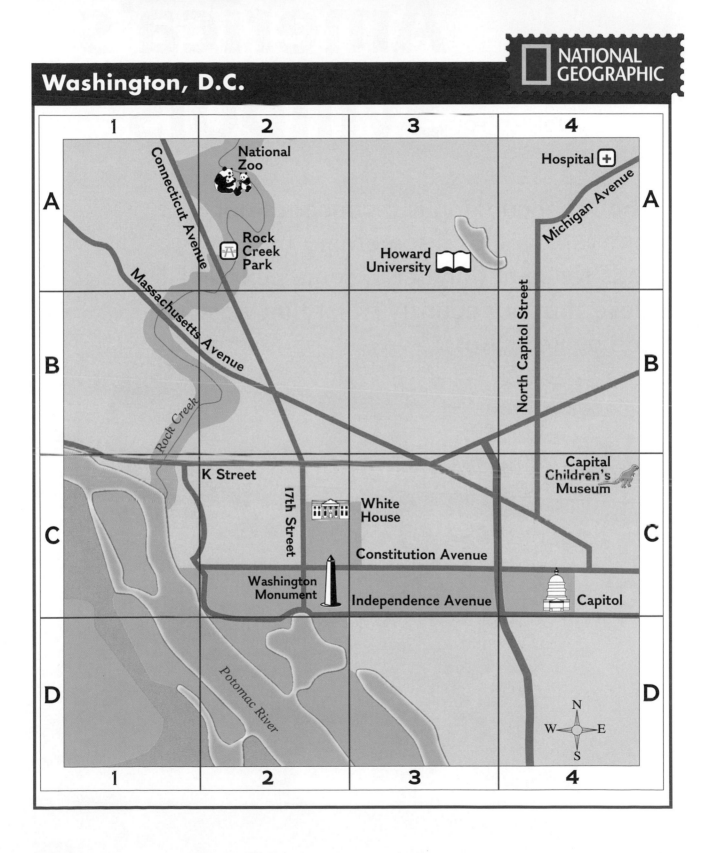

Washington, D.C.

NATIONAL GEOGRAPHIC

National Zoo

Rock Creek Park

Connecticut Avenue

Massachusetts Avenue

Rock Creek

Howard University

Hospital

Michigan Avenue

North Capitol Street

K Street

17th Street

White House

Constitution Avenue

Washington Monument

Independence Avenue

Capital Children's Museum

Capitol

Potomac River

N
W   E
S

America's Symbols

The American flag is a symbol of our country. A symbol is something that stands for something else. Some people believe that our country's first flag was made by Betsy Ross.

Our flag has 13 stripes. Each stripe stands for one of the first 13 states.

Our flag also has 50 stars. The stars stand for our country's 50 states.

What do the 50 stars on our flag stand for?

Country Symbols

Our country has many other symbols. One of them is the Statue of Liberty in New York harbor. The Statue of Liberty stands for our country's freedom.

The bald eagle and rose are also symbols of our country.

Bald Eagle

Statue of Liberty

Rose

State Symbols

Each of our country's 50 states has its own symbols. Every state has its own state flag, state bird, and state flower.

Which state do the symbols on this page stand for?

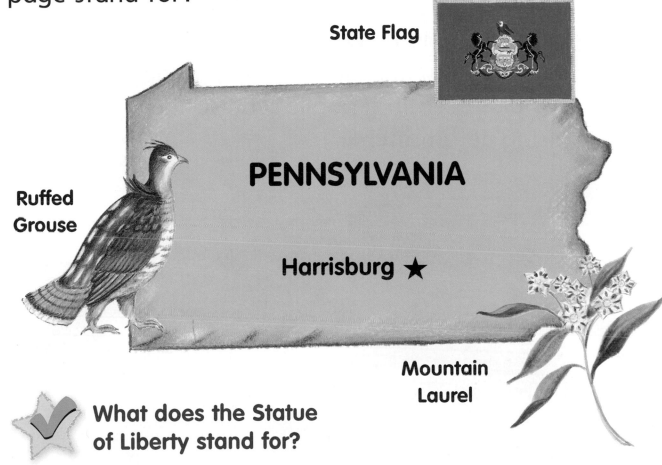

State Flag

PENNSYLVANIA

Ruffed Grouse

Harrisburg ★

Mountain Laurel

What does the Statue of Liberty stand for?

Think and Write!

1. Name four symbols of our country.

2. Do you think it is important for states to have symbols? Tell why or why not.

Celebrate America
with the Pledge

Francis Bellamy wrote the words to the Pledge of Allegiance. The pledge was first used in a public school flag raising ceremony.

The Pledge of Allegiance

by Francis Bellamy

I pledge allegiance to the flag
of the United States of America
and to the republic for which it stands,
one Nation under God, indivisible,
with liberty and justice for all.

Finding the Main Idea

The **main idea** tells what a paragraph is about. Read the paragraph below.

The red, white, and blue colors of the American flag have important meanings. Red stands for being brave. White stands for goodness. Blue stands for being fair.

The first sentence of this paragraph tells the main idea. This main idea is that the colors of the flag have important meanings. The other sentences in the paragraph tell more about the main idea. They tell what each color stands for.

Read this paragraph and then answer the questions.

Uncle Sam is a symbol of the United States. **U**ncle **S**am has the same first letters in his name, U.S., as in the **U**nited **S**tates. Uncle Sam's clothes have stars and colors just like our flag.

Try The Skill

1. Which sentence tells the main idea of the paragraph?

2. Which sentences tell more about the main idea?

3. Add another sentence to the paragraph that tells about the main idea.

273

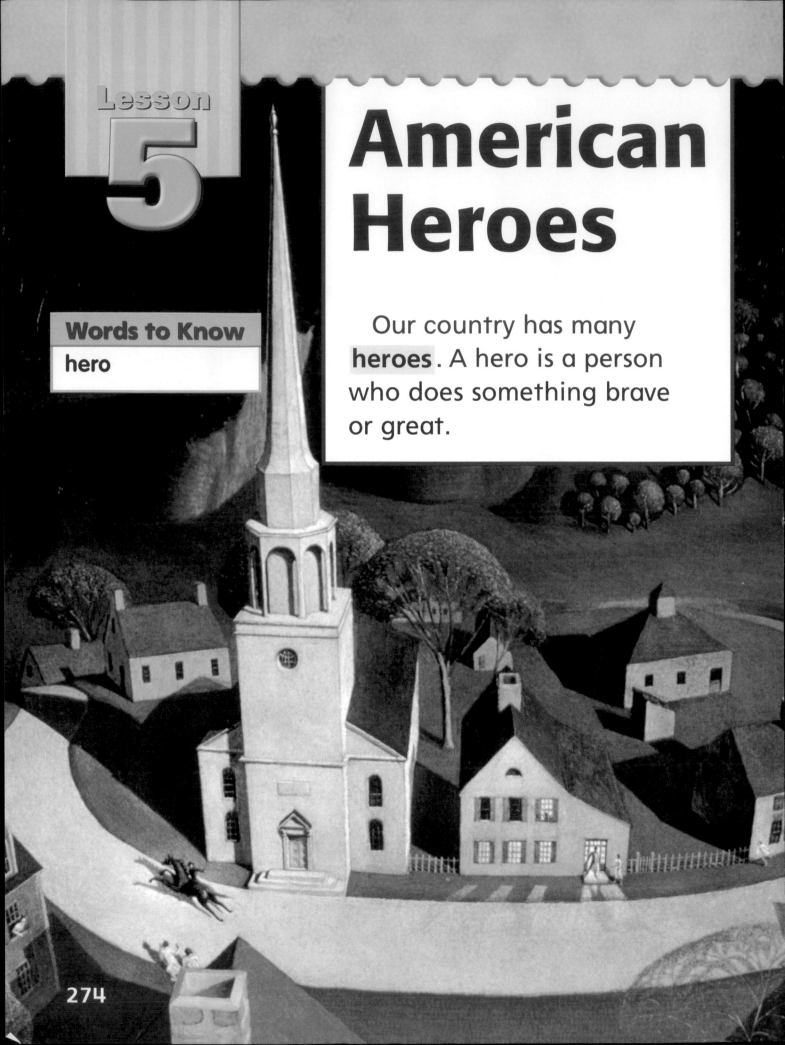

5

American Heroes

Words to Know

hero

Our country has many **heroes**. A hero is a person who does something brave or great.

274

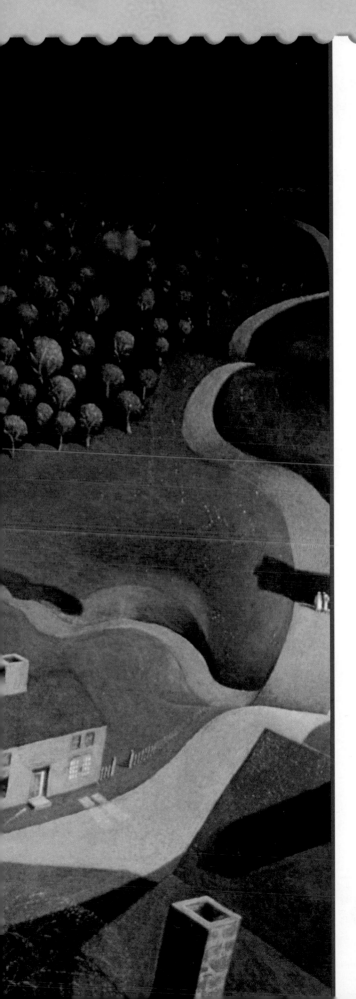

Many heroes have helped to make sure that Americans are free and that all Americans are treated fairly.

Paul Revere was a hero. He believed our country should be free from England. One night, he did something brave. He rode a horse from town to town to tell colonists that the English soldiers were coming. The soldiers caught him, but Paul Revere got away.

 How was Paul Revere brave?

Speaking Out

Americans often speak out for what they think is right. Susan B. Anthony did this. For many years women were not allowed to vote. Susan B. Anthony believed that America would be a better place if all people were treated equally. She worked hard to change the law so that women could vote. She led marches and gave speeches.

In her own words

"There will never be complete equality until women themselves help to make laws and elect lawmakers." —by *Susan B. Anthony*

Chief Joseph was a leader of the Nez Perce. The Nez Perce were Native Americans who lived in Oregon. Our government wanted to use this land for white settlers.

The Nez Perce thought this was unfair. They fought to keep their land. But they were forced to leave. Still, Chief Joseph kept speaking out for freedom. He went to Washington, D.C., and gave speeches. He said, "Let me be a free man, free to travel, free to stop, free to work, free to trade where I choose . . ."

What did Susan B. Anthony and Chief Joseph believe?

Working for Fairness

Americans like Rosa Parks have worked hard for fairness. Years ago, there were unfair laws in Montgomery, Alabama. Black people had to give up their seats to white people on crowded buses. Rosa thought this was unfair. One day, she would not give up her seat to a white man. Police took her to jail.

Many people, including Dr. Martin Luther King, Jr., agreed with Rosa Parks. Dr. King told the people of Montgomery to stop riding buses until the law was changed. People walked to work or school for one whole year. Finally, the law was changed.

Cesar Chavez and Dolores Huerta worked together to make life better for farm workers. Laws said that farm workers did not have to be treated the same as other workers. Cesar Chavez and Dolores Huerta gave speeches and led marches to change these unfair laws.

Today, Dolores Huerta still works to help others. She gives speeches about treating women fairly.

 How did Rosa Parks, Martin Luther King, Jr., Cesar Chavez, and Dolores Huerta work for fairness?

Many Ways to Be a Hero

John Glenn has been a soldier, astronaut, and government leader. When he was a young man, he was the first American to go around Earth in a spaceship. This was a very brave thing to do. Later, he was a senator for the state of Ohio. Senators make laws for our country. When he was 77 years old, John Glenn went into space again. He rode on the space shuttle *Discovery*. He is the oldest person ever to go into space!

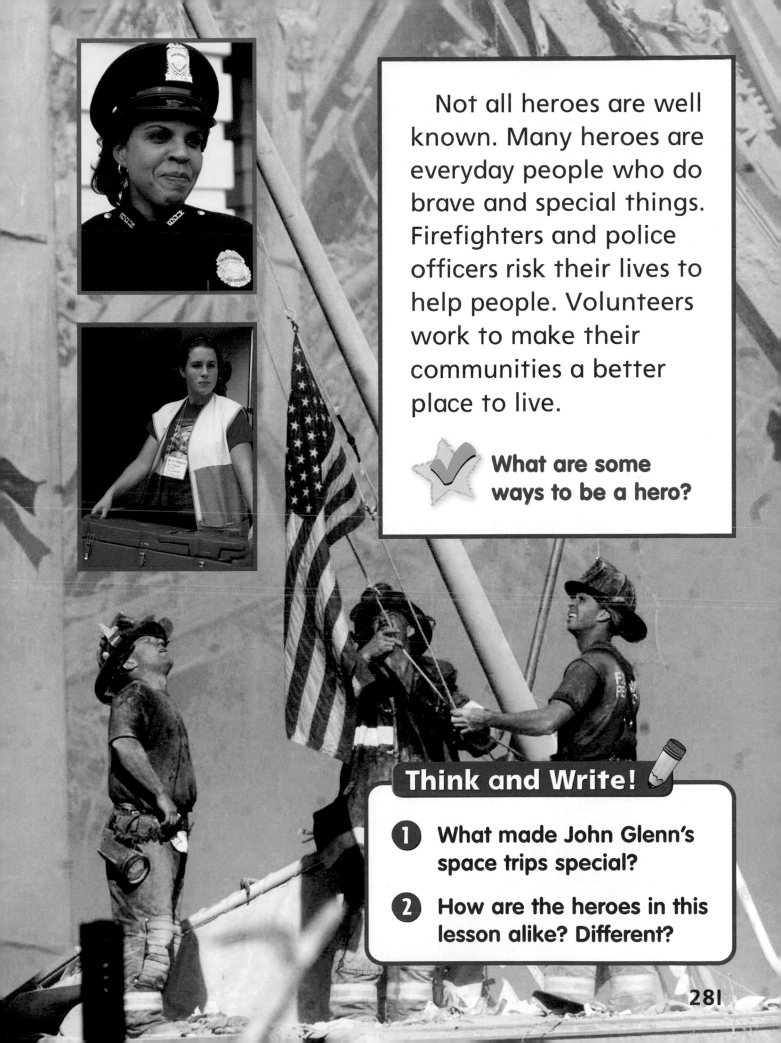

Not all heroes are well known. Many heroes are everyday people who do brave and special things. Firefighters and police officers risk their lives to help people. Volunteers work to make their communities a better place to live.

What are some ways to be a hero?

Think and Write!

1 What made John Glenn's space trips special?

2 How are the heroes in this lesson alike? Different?

The World Around Us

A Look at Government in Europe

Some countries in Europe decided to work closely together. The countries formed a group called the European Union. These countries keep their own laws. But together they also follow special European Union laws.

Most of the countries in the European Union use the same kind of money, called the *Euro*. This makes it easier for people to travel and do things in each other's country.

Talk about it!

Why do countries in the European Union use the same kind of money?

The map below shows the flags of the 15 countries that are in the European Union. It also shows the flag of the European Union.

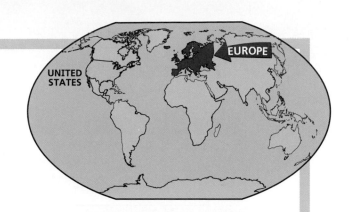

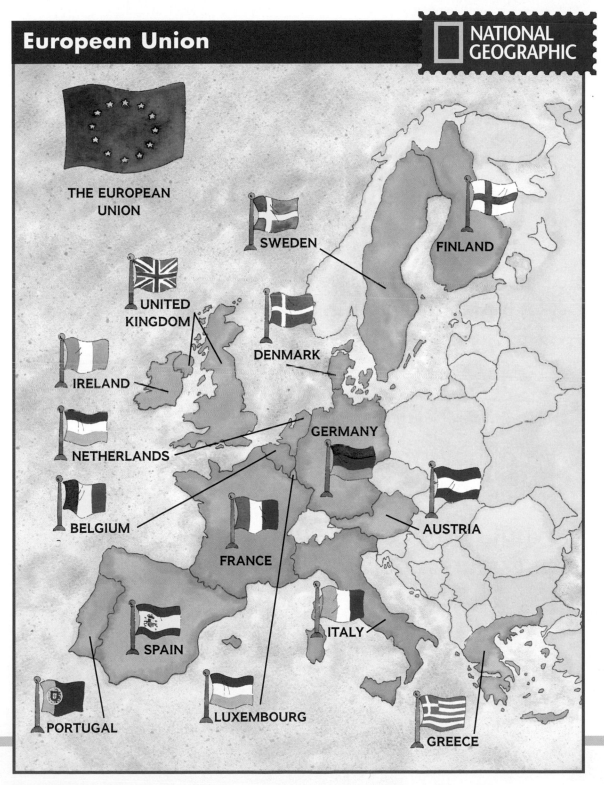

European Union

NATIONAL GEOGRAPHIC

THE EUROPEAN UNION

SWEDEN

FINLAND

UNITED KINGDOM

DENMARK

IRELAND

NETHERLANDS

GERMANY

BELGIUM

AUSTRIA

FRANCE

SPAIN

ITALY

PORTUGAL

LUXEMBOURG

GREECE

283

Words to Know

| monument government court |

Choose the word that best tells about each sentence.

1. This is the group of people in charge of running a community, state, or country.

2. This is a building or statue that shows special respect for a person or an event.

3. This is the place where people go to get help when they cannot agree about the law.

Check Your Reading

4. What does it mean to appoint a person to a job?

5. What do the members of Congress do at the Capitol?

6. Why would you need to be brave to change an unfair law?

Use a Grid Map

7. Put your finger on square A1. Move your finger right to square A2. What is in this square?

8. Now move your finger down to the Statue of Liberty. What square is it in?

Make a grid map of a city. Put City Hall and a Court House on your map.

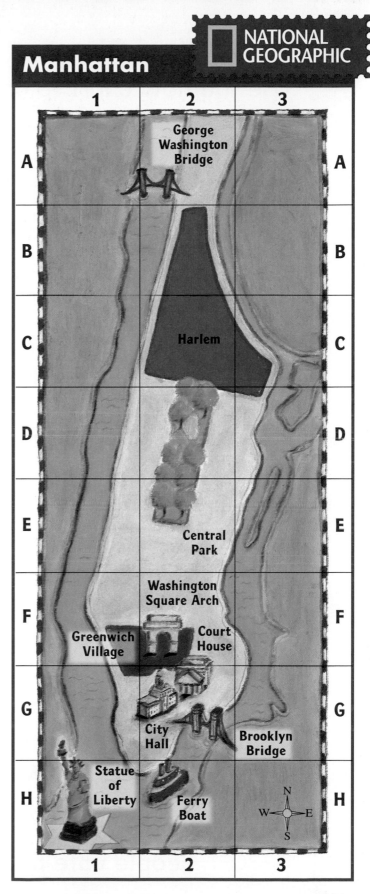

Use a Flow Chart

Use the flow chart to answer the question.

1. **Two people run for mayor.** 2. **People vote.** 3. **A mayor is elected.**

9. What happens just before a mayor is elected?

Find the Main Idea

TEST PREP

Read the paragraph to find the main idea.

> There are different ways to vote. For some elections people use machines to vote. Sometimes people vote by writing down their choice on paper. An easy way to vote is to just raise a hand!

10. What is the main idea of the paragraph?

⬭ There are different ways to vote.

⬭ People use machines to vote.

⬭ People vote by writing on paper.

Activity

Have a Class Election

* ❋ Have an election to choose a class flower.
* ❋ Write your vote on paper.
* ❋ Count the votes.
* ❋ Draw a picture of the winning flower.

Think and Write

Think about what you might want to know before you vote for someone. Write about it.

For more information about this unit, visit our Web site at **www.mhschool.com**

Celebrate Holidays

We celebrate holidays every year. Labor Day and Memorial Day honor America's people. Martin Luther King, Jr., Day and Presidents' Day, honor famous Americans. Independence Day celebrates freedom. Cinco de Mayo celebrates the Battle of Puebla.

Labor Day

On Labor Day we show respect for our country's working people. It is celebrated on the first Monday in September. Some cities have parades. Many people celebrate this day with a picnic.

Activity Make a Mobile

* Label a strip of paper "Happy Labor Day."
* Staple the strip into a circle.
* Draw four pictures of workers.
* On the back of each picture write what the worker does.
* Tie yarn to the top of each picture.
* Staple the yarn to the paper circle.
* Hang up high.

Thanksgiving

Thanksgiving Day is celebrated on the fourth Thursday in November. We remember the feast shared by the Pilgrims and the Native Americans on this day.

On Thanksgiving Day we give thanks for what we have. We share a big meal with family and friends.

I am thankful for...

Food to eat

My family

My house

My Kitten

Activity

Create a Class Collage

* Draw a picture of something you are thankful for.

* Write a label under your picture.

* Paste everyone's pictures onto a large sheet of paper.

Martin Luther King, Jr., Day

Martin Luther King, Jr., Day is celebrated on the third Monday in January. Martin Luther King, Jr., helped to change laws that were unfair to African Americans. He led marches and gave speeches. On this day, we remember his dream for all people to live together in peace. We celebrate this holiday with parades and speeches.

Activity Write About Your Dreams

* Cut out two large cloud shapes.
* On the clouds, write about dreams that you have for the world.

> I dream that all people have food to eat.

> I dream that people are kind to each other all over the world.

Presidents' Day

Presidents' Day is on the third Monday in February. On this day, we celebrate the work of two Presidents, George Washington and Abraham Lincoln. Schools, banks, and many offices are closed to show respect for these two great American leaders.

Activity

Make a Postage Stamp

❋ Draw a picture of Washington or Lincoln.

❋ Add a design to the stamp.

❋ On the back of the stamp, write a few sentences about the President you drew.

Cinco de Mayo

Cinco de Mayo means "fifth of May" in Spanish. This holiday celebrates the day in 1862 when Mexico won the Battle of Puebla against France. It celebrates the courage of the Mexican Army. This holiday is celebrated with parades, parties, and speeches.

Activity   Create a Poster

* Write a Spanish saying on your poster, such as "Viva la libertad!" (Long live liberty!)
* Add pictures of a Cinco de Mayo celebration and the Mexican flag.

Memorial Day

Memorial Day is celebrated on the last Monday in May. On this day, we show respect for the soldiers who died in our country's wars. Many people celebrate this holiday by going to parades or visiting war memorials.

Activity

Make a Memorial Day Wreath

* Make a flower out of colorful tissue paper.
* Attach or paste the flower to a piece of cardboard shaped like a wreath.
* Attach a message under the wreath.

We remember our heroes.

Independence Day

Independence Day, or the Fourth of July, honors our country's birthday. We remember that on July 4, 1776, we declared our freedom. We celebrate with parades and fireworks to show that we are proud to be Americans.

Activity Play a Matching Game

* Draw Fourth of July symbols on index cards such as the Liberty Bell, fireworks, the flag, or an eagle.

* Write matching words that name the symbols on index cards.

* Play the matching game with a partner.

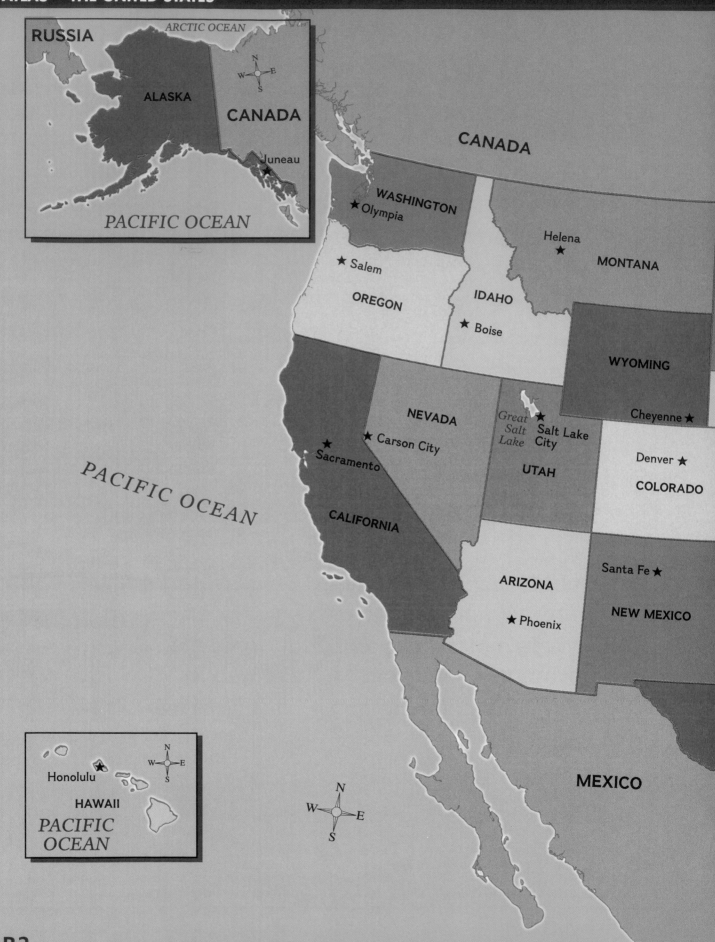

RUSSIA

ARCTIC OCEAN

ALASKA

CANADA

N
W E
S

Juneau

PACIFIC OCEAN

CANADA

WASHINGTON
★ Olympia

Helena
★

MONTANA

★ Salem

OREGON

IDAHO

★ Boise

WYOMING

Cheyenne ★

NEVADA

★ Carson City

Great
Salt
Lake

Salt Lake
City
★

PACIFIC OCEAN

★
Sacramento

UTAH

Denver ★

COLORADO

CALIFORNIA

ARIZONA

Santa Fe ★

★ Phoenix

NEW MEXICO

Honolulu ★

N
W E
S

HAWAII
PACIFIC
OCEAN

N
W E
S

MEXICO

CANADA

Lake Superior

NORTH DAKOTA
★ Bismarck

MINNESOTA

St. Paul ★

SOUTH DAKOTA
★ Pierre

WISCONSIN

Madison ★

Lake Michigan

MICHIGAN

Lansing ★

Lake Huron

Lake Erie

Lake Ontario

MAINE
Augusta ★

VERMONT
Montpelier ★

NEW HAMPSHIRE
★ Concord

Albany ★

MASSACHUSETTS
★ Boston

NEW YORK

Hartford ★ **CONNECTICUT**

★ Providence
RHODE ISLAND

IOWA
★ Des Moines

NEBRASKA
Lincoln ★

ILLINOIS

Springfield ★

Indianapolis ★

INDIANA

OHIO

Columbus ★

PENNSYLVANIA
Harrisburg ★

★ Trenton
NEW JERSEY

Dover ★ **DELAWARE**

Washington, D.C. ★ Annapolis
MARYLAND

WEST VIRGINIA
★ Charleston

Richmond ★

VIRGINIA

Topeka ★

KANSAS

MISSOURI
★ Jefferson City

Frankfort ★

KENTUCKY

Nashville ★

NORTH CAROLINA ★ Raleigh

OKLAHOMA
★ Oklahoma City

ARKANSAS

Little Rock ★

TENNESSEE

SOUTH CAROLINA
★ Columbia

Atlanta ★

ATLANTIC OCEAN

MISSISSIPPI

Jackson ★

ALABAMA

Montgomery ★

GEORGIA

TEXAS

LOUISIANA

Baton Rouge ★

★ Austin

★ Tallahassee

FLORIDA

Gulf of Mexico

THE BAHAMAS

⊛ **National capital**   ★ **State capital**

CUBA

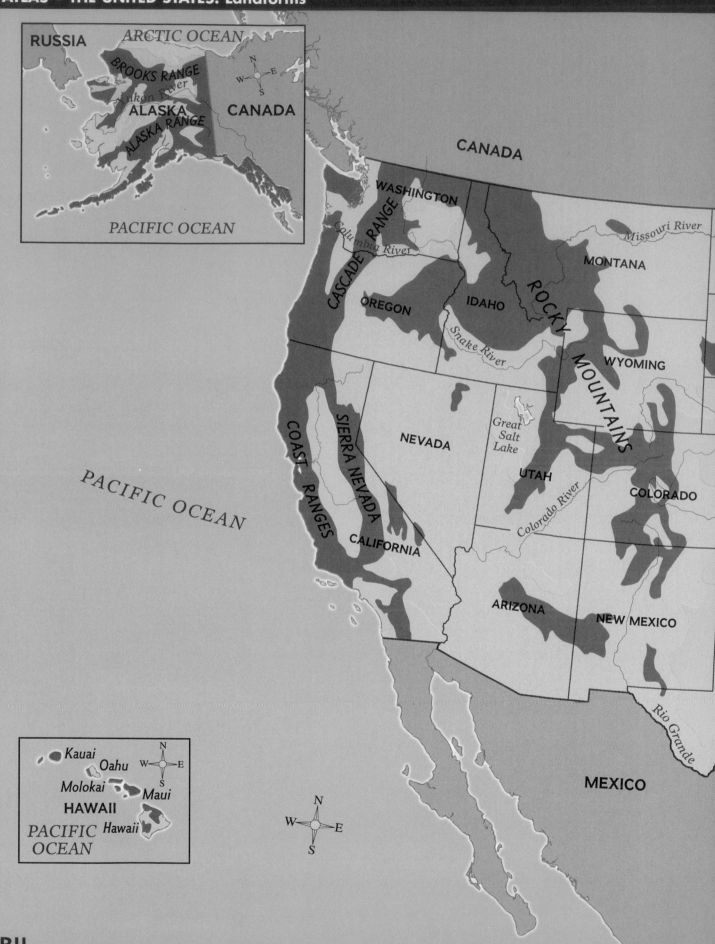

NATIONAL GEOGRAPHIC

CANADA

NORTH DAKOTA

MINNESOTA

Lake Superior

MAINE

VERMONT

NEW HAMPSHIRE

MICHIGAN

Lake Huron

Lake Ontario

NEW YORK

MASSACHUSETTS

SOUTH DAKOTA

WISCONSIN

Lake Michigan

Lake Erie

CONNECTICUT

RHODE ISLAND

PENNSYLVANIA

NEW JERSEY

DELAWARE

MARYLAND

NEBRASKA

IOWA

Platte River

Wabash River

OHIO

MOUNTAINS

GREAT PLAINS

ILLINOIS

INDIANA

Ohio River

Washington, D.C.

WEST VIRGINIA

VIRGINIA

KANSAS

MISSOURI

Mississippi River

KENTUCKY

NORTH CAROLINA

APPALACHIAN

COASTAL PLAIN

ATLANTIC OCEAN

OZARK PLATEAU

TENNESSEE

Tennessee River

Arkansas River

OKLAHOMA

ARKANSAS

SOUTH CAROLINA

Savannah River

ATLANTIC

Red River

MISSISSIPPI

ALABAMA

GEORGIA

LOUISIANA

TEXAS

GULF   COASTAL   PLAIN

FLORIDA

Gulf of Mexico

THE BAHAMAS

Mountains   Hills   Plains

★ National capital

CUBA

R5

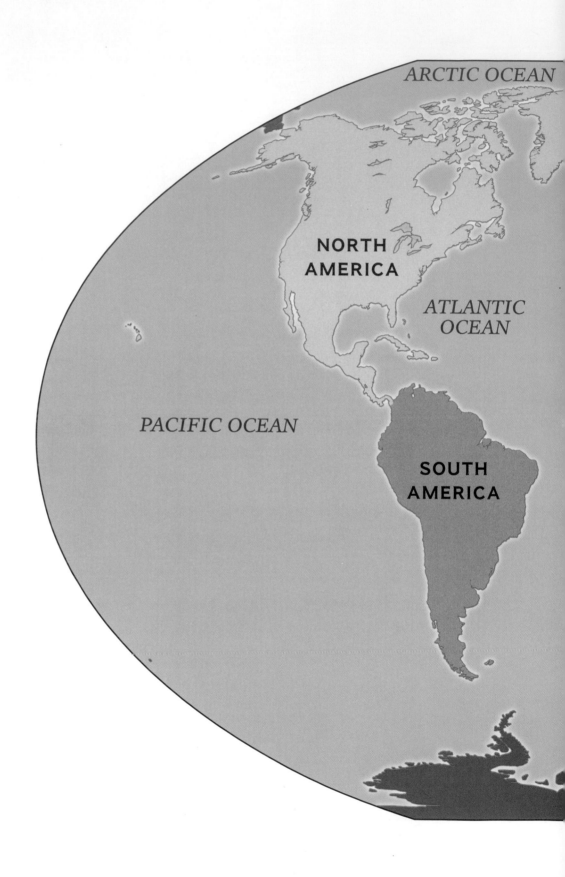

ARCTIC OCEAN

NORTH
AMERICA

ATLANTIC
OCEAN

PACIFIC OCEAN

SOUTH
AMERICA

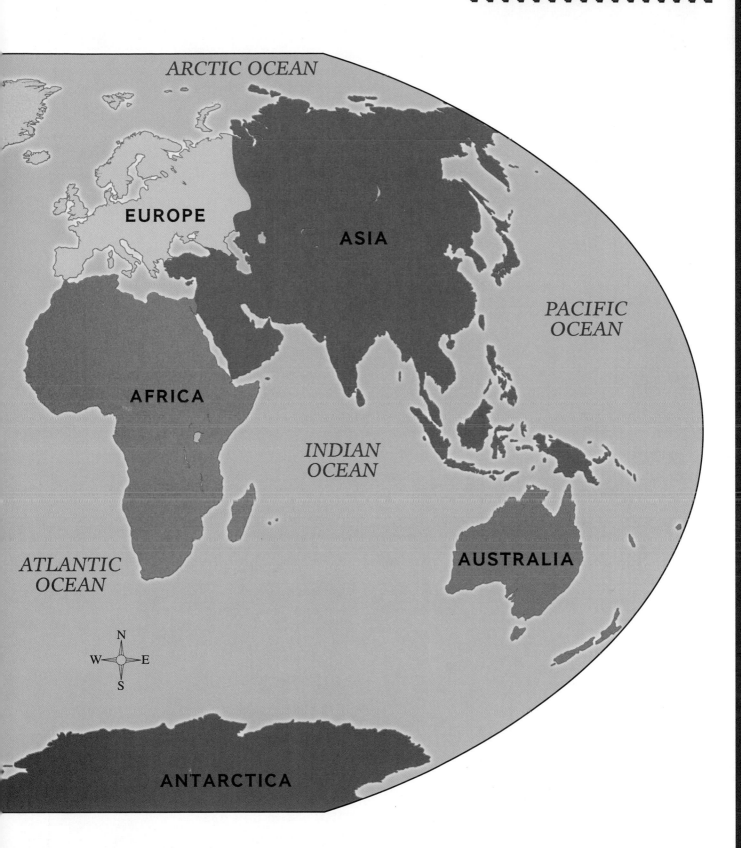

NATIONAL
GEOGRAPHIC

ARCTIC OCEAN

EUROPE

ASIA

PACIFIC
OCEAN

AFRICA

INDIAN
OCEAN

ATLANTIC
OCEAN

AUSTRALIA

N
W—E
S

ANTARCTICA

Dictionary of Geographic Words

HILL—Land that is higher than the land around it, but lower than a mountain.

PENINSULA—Land that has water on all sides but one.

LAKE—Body of water with land all around it.

PLAIN—Flat land.

ISLAND—Land that has water all around it.

MOUNTAIN—Highest kind of land.

VALLEY—Low land between hills or mountains.

RIVER—Single stream of water that flows into an ocean or lake.

OCEAN—Very large body of salt water.

Picture Glossary

A

ancient times Times that happened very long ago. This tool was used for hunting in **ancient times.** (page 164)

C

capital A city where leaders of a country or state work. The **capital** of North Carolina is Raleigh. (page 70)

Capitol The building where people who work for Congress meet. I took a picture of the **Capitol** on our trip. (page 261)

---

citizen A member of a community, state, or country. Good **citizens** help to keep their community clean. (page 38)

---

colonist A person who lives in a colony. Squanto showed the **colonists** how to grow their own food. (page 137)

---

colony A place that is ruled by another country. Plymouth was once a **colony** of England. (page 137)

communication The way people share ideas, thoughts, or information with each other. Many people use telephones for **communication.** (page 32)

community A place where people live, work, and have fun together. The **community** I live in is a small town. (page 8)

consumer Someone who uses the goods made by a producer. The **consumer** bought many fruits and vegetables. (page 203)

continent A very large body of land. There are seven **continents** on Earth. (page H13)

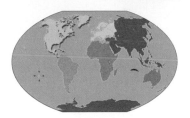

country A land and the people who live there. Our **country** is the United States of America. (page H11)

United States of America

court A place where people go to get help when they cannot agree about the law. Judges work in a **court.** (page 247)

D

direction Any way you face or point. A compass rose shows the four main **directions.** They are north, south, east, and west. (page H14)

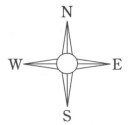

Picture Glossary

E

earn To get paid money for work you do. I rake leaves to **earn** money. (page 184)

election A special time when we vote for our leaders. We have an **election** every four years to choose our President. (page 244)

explorer A person who travels to a new place to learn about it. An astronaut is an **explorer.** (page 132)

F

factory A building where things are made. Some goods are made in a **factory.** (page 209)

G

geography The study of Earth and the people, plants, and animals that live on Earth. I am studying **geography** when I learn about continents. (page 66)

globe A model of Earth. Our teacher showed us land and water on the **globe.** (page H13)

goods Things made or grown. The people in the community buy **goods** at the store. (page 196)

government The group of people who run a community, state, or country. A community board is one part of community **government.** (page 238)

governor The leader of a state. The **governor** makes sure that the laws of the state are followed. (page 243)

H

hill Land that is higher than land around it, but not as high as a mountain. We walked up the **hill.** (page 78)

history The story of the past. I can learn about my country's **history.** (page 122)

I

immigrant A person who leaves one country to live in another. My grandmother is an **immigrant** from China. (page 160)

independence To be free from other people or places. On the Fourth of July, we celebrate our country's **independence.** (page 144)

interview To ask a person questions and write down the answers. I **interviewed** my neighbor about El Paso. (page 48)

Picture Glossary

island Land that has water going all the way around it. The **island** has many trees. (page 77)

lake A body of water with land all around it. We fish in the **lake.** (page 80)

landform One of the different shapes of land on Earth. Mountains, hills, and plains are **landforms.** (page 77)

law A rule we must all follow. Some **laws** are shown on signs. (page 37)

legend A story that has been told for many years. The teacher told the class the **legend** of the bluebonnet. (page 50)

M

map A drawing of a place. The **map** shows landforms in Oklahoma. (page H9)

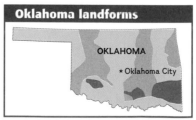

Oklahoma landforms

OKLAHOMA

★ Oklahoma City

map key Tells what the symbols on a map mean. The **map key** shows that a star stands for the state capital. (page H10)

■ Mountains
■ Hills
■ Plains

★ State capital

mayor The leader of a community. The **mayor** makes sure that laws are followed in a community. (page 243)

modern times Times that are happening now, or times that happened a short while ago. In **modern times,** we use cars for transportation. (page 166)

monument A building or statue that shows special respect for a person or an event. The Washington **Monument** is in Washington, D.C. (page 260)

mountain The highest form of land. There is snow on the top of the **mountain.** (page 78)

museum A place that keeps things for people to see and learn about. I learned about hot air balloons at the children's **museum.** (page 15)

N

Native Americans The first people to live in America. **Native Americans** are also called American Indians. (page 126)

natural resource Something in nature that people use. Sunlight and soil are **natural resources.** (page 93)

Picture Glossary

needs Things people must have to live. Food, clothes, shelter, and love are **needs.** (page 194)

neighbor A person who lives close to another. My mother talks over the fence to our **neighbor.** (page 12)

o

ocean A very large body of salt water. We live near the Atlantic **Ocean.** (page H13)

P

peninsula Land that has water on all sides but one. One of the sides of a **peninsula** is joined to a larger body of land. (page 77)

pioneer A person who leads the way into land he or she does not know. Many **pioneers** traveled in covered wagons. (page 158)

plain A flat area of land. Most **plains** are good for growing vegetables. (page 78)

President The leader of our country. Abraham Lincoln was our sixteenth **President.** (page 145)

producer Someone who makes or grows goods to sell. A farmer is a **producer.** (page 202)

R

recycle Make fit to be used again. My family **recycles** cans. (page 105)

river A single stream of water that flows into an ocean or lake. Snake **River** flows into the Pacific Ocean. (page 80)

rural area An area that is made up mostly of farmland. My uncle's farm is in a **rural area.** (page 24)

S

season One of the four different times of the year. The four **seasons** are spring, summer, fall, and winter. (page 87)

service Something useful that people do for others. One **service** a doctor does is to help people when they are sick. (page 197)

shelter A place where people live. Our house is a **shelter**. (page 194)

Picture Glossary

slavery One person owning another. Many people went north to escape from **slavery.** (page 152)

state A part of a country. The **state** of Florida is one part of the United States. (page H12)

suburb A community that is near a city. Many families live in a **suburb.** (page 22)

symbol Something that stands for something else. The Statue of Liberty is a **symbol** of freedom. (page H10)

T

tax Money that people pay to the community. Firefighters are paid with **tax** money from the community. (page 187)

technology Using science to make things faster, easier, or better. Computer **technology** has made it easier to find information. (page 220)

trade To give something and then get something back. The United States and Japan **trade** goods. (page 214)

tradition A special way of doing something that is passed down over time. A Thanksgiving Day parade is an American **tradition** in many cities. (page 128)

transportation A way of moving people or things from one place to another. A car is a kind of **transportation.** (page 30)

U

urban area A city and the places around it. **Urban areas** have tall buildings and busy streets. (page 20)

V

valley Low land between mountains or hills. We walked down to the floor of the **valley.** (page 78)

volunteer A person who works but is not paid. Some **volunteers** serve food to homeless people. (page 188)

W

wants Things people would like to have but do not need in order to live. Games and toys are **wants.** (page 195)

White House The place where the President lives and works. The **White House** is in Washington, D.C. (page 262)

Index

Credits

All photographs are by Macmillan/McGraw-Hill (MMH) and Ken Karp for MMH except as noted below:

Cover; A17: t.r. John M. Roberts/Corbis Stock Market; bkgd Joe Sohm, Visions of America/Pan America; b. AGI Photographic Imaging.

National Edition, page A1: bdr. PhotoLink/Photo Disc. A1: clockwise from t.l.: ©Michael Krasowitz/FPG International; ©Jerry Tobias/Corbis; ©Simon Wilkinson/The Image Bank; ©Elyse Lewin Studio Inc./The Image Bank; ©LWA-Dann Tardif/Corbis Stock Market; ©Ghislain & Marie David de Lossy/The Image Bank; b.r. ©AJA Productions/The Image Bank; ©Ross Whitaker/The Image Bank; b.l. ©Vicky Kasala/The Image Bank; ©Vicky Kasala/The Image Bank; ©LWA-Dann Tardif/Corbis Stock Market; c. ©Elyse Lewin Studio Inc./The Image Bank.

Texas Edition, page A1: Row 1: (1) ©Bob Daemmrich Photography, Inc., (2) ©Superstock, (3) ©Max Spitzenberger/Bob Daemmrich Photography, Inc., (4) ©Bob Daemmrich Photography, Inc., (5) ©John Bova/Photo Researchers, Inc., (6) ©Bob Daemmrich Photography, Inc., (7) ©Bob Daemmrich Photography, Inc., (8) ©Superstock; **Row 2:** (1) ©Max Spitzenberger/Bob Daemmrich Photography, Inc., (2) ©Jeff Lepore/Photo Researchers, Inc., (3) ©Bob Daemmrich Photography, Inc., (4) ©Jeff Lepore/Photo Researchers, Inc., (5) ©John Bova/Photo Researchers, Inc., (6) ©Bob Daemmrich Photography, Inc., (7) ©Jeff Lepore/Photo Researchers, Inc., (8) ©John Bova/Photo Researchers, Inc., (9) ©Bob Daemmrich Photography, Inc., (10) ©Max Spitzenberger/Bob Daemmrich Photography, Inc.; **Row 3:** (1) ©Bob Daemmrich Photography, Inc., (2) ©Leo Touchet/Woodfin Camp and Associates, (3) ©John Bova/Photo Researchers, Inc., (4) ©Bob Daemmrich Photography, Inc., (5) ©Max Spitzenberger/Bob Daemmrich Photography, Inc., (6) ©John Bova/Photo Researchers, Inc., (7) ©Bob Daemmrich Photography, Inc., (8) ©Bob Daemmrich Photography, Inc., (9) ©Walter Bibikow/Folio, Inc., (10) ©Gregory T. Martin/Superstock; **Row 4:** (1) ©Leo Touchet/Woodfin Camp and Associates, (2) ©Bob Daemmrich Photography, Inc., (3) ©Jeff Lepore/Photo Researchers, Inc., (4) ©Walter Bibikow/Folio, Inc., (5) ©Superstock, (6) ©Bob Daemmrich Photography, Inc., (7) ©Walter Bibikow/Folio, Inc., (8) ©Max Spitzenberger/Bob Daemmrich Photography, Inc., (9) ©Jeff Lepore/Photo Researchers, Inc., (10) ©Leo Touchet/Woodfin Camp and Associates; **Row 5:** (1) ©Jeff Lepore/Photo Researchers, Inc., (2) ©Max Spitzenberger/Bob Daemmrich Photography, Inc., (3) ©Bob Daemmrich Photography, Inc., (4) ©Superstock, (6) ©Gregory T. Martin/Superstock, (7) ©Jeff Lepore/Photo Researchers, Inc., (8) ©Gregory T. Martin/Superstock, (9) ©Bob Daemmrich Photography, Inc., ©John Bova/Photo Researchers, Inc.; **Row 6:** (1) ©Superstock, (2) ©John Bova/Photo Researchers, Inc., (3) ©Gregory T. Martin/Superstock, (4) ©Max Spitzenberger/Bob Daemmrich Photography, Inc., (7) ©Leo Touchet/Woodfin Camp and Associates, (8) ©Bob Daemmrich Photography, Inc., (9) ©Walter Bibikow/Folio, Inc., (10) ©Max Spitzenberger/Bob Daemmrich Photography, Inc.; **Row 7:** (1) ©Jeff Lepore/Photo Researchers, Inc., (2) ©Walter Bibikow/Folio, Inc., (3) ©Bob Daemmrich Photography, Inc., (4) ©Leo Touchet/Woodfin Camp and Associates, (5) ©Jeff Lepore/Photo Researchers, Inc., (7) ©Max Spitzenberger/Bob Daemmrich Photography, Inc., (8) ©John Bova/Photo Researchers, Inc., (9) ©Walter Bibikow/Folio, Inc., (10) ©Jeff Lepore/Photo Researchers, Inc.; **Row 8:** (1) ©Gregory T. Martin/Superstock, (2) ©Leo Touchet/Woodfin Camp and Associates, (3) ©Max Spitzenberger/Bob Daemmrich Photography, Inc., (4) ©Superstock, (5) ©Bob Daemmrich Photography, Inc., (6) ©Jeff Lepore/Photo Researchers, Inc., (7) ©Bob Daemmrich Photography, Inc., (8) ©Superstock, (9) ©Max Spitzenberger/Bob Daemmrich Photography, Inc., (10) ©Leo Touchet/Woodfin Camp and Associates; **Row 9:** (1) ©Bob Daemmrich Photo, (2) ©Bob Daemmrich/The Image Works, (3) ©Richard Sisk/Panoramic Images, (4) ©Bob Daemmrich Photo, (5) ©Bob Daemmrich/The Image Works, (6) ©Richard Sisk/Panoramic Images, (7) ©Bob Daemmrich Photo, (8) ©Bob Daemmrich/The Image Works, (9) ©Richard Sisk/Panoramic Images, (10) ©Bob Daemmrich Photo; **Row 10:** (1) ©Cathy & Gordon ILLG/Earth Scenes, (2) ©Charles W. Mann/Photo Researchers, Inc., (3) ©Ron Jautz/ Folio, Inc., (4) ©Cathy & Gordon ILLG/Earth Scenes, (5) ©Conrad Zobel/Corbis, (6) ©Bob Daemmrich Photo, (7) ©Charles W. Mann/Photo Researchers, Inc., (8) ©Conrad Zobel/Corbis, (9) ©Jeff Greenberg/Folio, Inc., (10) ©Cathy & Gordon ILLG/Earth Scenes; **Row 11:** (1) ©Superstock, (2) ©Jeff Greenberg/Folio, Inc., (3) ©Mary Steinbacher/PhotoEdit, (4) ©Charles W. Mann/Photo Researchers, Inc., (5) ©Ron Jautz/ Folio, Inc., (6) ©Cathy & Gordon ILLG/ Earth Scenes, (7) ©Jeff Greenberg/Folio, Inc., (8) ©Superstock, (9) ©Ron Jautz/Folio, Inc., (10) ©Charles W. Mann/Photo Researchers, Inc.; Row 12: (1) ©Ron Jautz/Folio, Inc., (2) ©Conrad Zobel/Corbis, (3) ©Cathy & Gordon ILLG/Earth Scenes, (4) ©Superstock, (5) ©Jeff Greenberg/Folio, Inc., (6) ©Mary Steinbacher/PhotoEdit, (7) ©Charles W. Mann/Photo Researchers, Inc., (8) ©Conrad Zobel/Corbis, (9) ©Mary Steinbacher/PhotoEdit, (10) ©Jeff Greenberg/Folio, Inc.; mm. ©Bob Daemmrich/The Image Works. **Section A:** A2: t.r. Getty Images; A3: t.r. ©Joseph Sohm/Visions of America/ Corbis; b.l. National Archives; A6-7: bkgd Jim Cummins/FPG; A8: ©Bettmann/Corbis; br., Associated Press, AP. A9: ©Bettmann/Corbis. A10: tr., ©Kevin Fleming/Corbis; b., ©Roger Markham-Smith/ International Stock. A11: tr., ©Tecmap Corporation; Eric Curry/Corbis; bl., ©1993 David Ulmer/ Stock Boston; mr., ©Nasa/ Science Photo Library/ Photo Researchers, Inc.; A12: bl., Rob Crandall/Stock Boston; br., ©Bettmann/Corbis; tl., ©Joseph Sohm; Visions of America/Corbis; ml., ©AFP/Corbis; tr., ©Royalty Free/ Corbis. A13: ©Associated Press, AP; bl., The Granger Collection. A14: br., ©Bob Daemmrich/ Stock Boston/ PictureQuest; Spencer Grant/Stock Boston. A15: tr., ©Margaret Carson Revis; br., ©Mickey Pfleger/ Photo 20-20/ PictureQuest; bl., ©Mickey Pfleger/ Photo 20-20/ PictureQuest. A16: t., ©Bettmann/Corbis; mt., ©Cindy Lewis Photography; mb., ©Bettmann/Corbis; b., ©2001 General Motors Corporation. Used with permission of GM Media Archives; ©Bob Daemmrich/ Stock Boston, Inc/PictureQuest. [Texas Edition: A8: br. Daemmrich/The Image Works; tr. Superstock; tl. Gilcrease Museum, Tulsa; br. Joel Salcido/Daemmrich Photo Associates; bl. Tom & Pat Leeson/Photo Reseachers, Inc.; A9: bl. Leo Touchet/Woodfin Camp & Associates; tr. Harry Cabluck/Associated Press, AP; tl. Bettmann/Corbis; tm. Nasa/Science Photo Library/ Photo Researchers, Inc.; br. Bob Daemmrich/Bob Daemmrich Photo, Inc.; A10: tr. Jim Zipp 1999/Photo Researchers, Inc.; bl. Roger Markham-Smith International Stock. b. Joe McDonald/Visuals Unlimited; A11: b. Kelvin Aitken/Peter Arnold, Inc.; mr. B. Daemmrich/The Image Works; A12: tr. John Sohlden/Visuals Unlimited; b. Richard R. Hansen/Photo Researchers, Inc.; ml. Jan Halaska/Photo Researchers, Inc.; mr. Tim Heneghan/Index Stock Imagery; A13: bkgd Daemmrich/The Image Works; br. Leo Touchet/Woodfin Camp and Associates; A14: bkgd. Reuters NewMedia Inc./Corbis; mr. AFP/Corbis; A15: br. Joseph Scherschel/TimePix; bkgd. Courtesy of Adair Margo Gallery; tr. Art Collection, Harry Ransom Humanities Research Center, The University of Texas at Austin; A16: tr. Ann Purcell/Photo Researchers; bkgd. Alfred Pasieka/Science Photo Library/Photo Researchers, Inc.; mr. Bob Daemmrich.] **Section H:** H1: tl Kevin Kolczynski for MMH; bl. Craig Tuttle/The Stock Market; tr. Michael Newman/Photo Edit; br. Richard T. Nowitz / Photo Researchers; H2: br. Jose L. Pelaez/The Stock Market; br. Jose L. Pelaez/The Stock Market; tl. Steve Chenn/Corbis; bl. NASA; tr. Fil Hunter for MMH; H5: mr. Barrie Rokeach/Barrie Rokeach; H6: m. Chuck Pefley/Stock Boston; H7: tl. Joe Atlas/Brand X Pictures/PictureQuest; br. Jeff Greenberg/Folio, Inc.; l. Dennis Johnson/Folio, Inc.; tr. AP/Wide World Photos; H8: b. Digital Vision/PictureQuest; t. Catherine Karnow/Folio, Inc.; m. Joseph H. Bailey; H9: b. Austin Brown/Stone; H13: bl. Tom Van Sant/Stock Market; H14: m. David Mager for MMH. 6-7: m. Lawrence Migdale; bkgrd Rhoda Sidney/Photo Edit; 8: r. Billy Barnes/Stock Boston; 9: bl. David Young-Wolff/Photo Edit; t. Peter Vandermark/Stock Boston; 12: ml. Dennis Cox/D.E. Cox Photo Library; 13: mr. Dennis Cox/D.E. Cox Photo Library; 14-15: m. Dennis Cox/D.E. Cox Photo Library; 16: bl. Dennis Cox/D.E. Cox Photo Library; 17: tr. University Productions; 20-21: bkgrd Richard Nowitz/National Geographic; 22: m. Stephen Knox/The Knox Files; 23: m. Rachel Epstein/Photo Edit; 24-25: bkgrd Stephen Knox/The Knox Files; 25: t. Waverley Traylor/Waverley Traylor Photography; tr. Town of Smithfield, VA; 30-31: Corbis; 31: tr. The Granger Collection; 32: m. Corbis; br. Hulton Archive; 33: r. Bob Daemmrich/Stock Boston; b. Adam Smith/FPG International; 34-35: bkgrd, b. Archive Photos; t. Billy Barnes/Stock Boston; 37: tr. Tony Freeman/Photo Edit; br. Michael Newman/Photo Edit; inset D. Young-Wolf/Photo Edit; 38: tl. N.K. Denny/Photo Edit; 38-39: b. Michael Gadomski/Dembinsky Photo Associates; 39: tr. Frank Siteman/Stock Boston; 40: t. Corbis; bl. AP/Wide World Photos; 40-41: m. AP/Wide World Photos; 41: bm. Paul Thompson/Archive Photos; 51: br. Bob Daemmrich/Stock Boston; mr. William Johnson/Stock Boston; 52: ml. Sheila McKinnon/Mira; b. Sheila McKinnon/Mira; 53: r. K Adle/The Aga Khan Trust for Culture; 54: br. Corbis; 64: bkgrd David Nunuk/Photo Researchers, Inc.; tr. NASA; 65: m WorldSat International /Science Source/Photo Researchers, Inc.; 77: l. Chuck Pefley/Stock Boston; r. Barrie Rokeach; 79: tl. John Elk III/Stock Boston; tr. David Simson/PictureQuest; br. John Elk III/Bruce Coleman, Inc.; 80: l. John Elk III/Stock Boston; 81: tl. John Elk III/Stock Boston; r. C C Lockwood/Bruce Coleman, Inc.; 84: b. Stephen Graham/Dembinsky Photo Associates; m. Tom Bean/Tony Stone Images; 85: t. Darrell Gulin/Dembinsky Photo Associates; 87: tl. bkgrd Jan Halaska/Photo Researchers, Inc.; tr. Jan Halaska/Photo Researchers, Inc.; bl. Jan Halaska/Photo Researchers, Inc.; br. Jan Halaska/Photo Researchers, Inc.; 88-89: bkgrd Wendell Metzen/Bruce Coleman, Inc.; 89: ml. West Coast Shutters; mr. Tom McCarthy/Photo Edit; 92-93: bkgrd Carr Clifton/Minden Pictures; 94: l. Scott T. Smith/Dembinsky Photo Associates; tr. C Squared Studio /PhotoDisc; 96-97: bkgrd Larry Dale Gordon/Getty; 97: m. Patti McConville/Dembinsky Photo Associates; 98: b. Patti McConville/Dembinsky Photo Associates; 98-99: bkgrd Chuck Pelfly/Stock Boston; 99: tr. Stock Boston; 101: r. Dembinsky Photo Associates; l. Rhoda Sidney/Stock Boston; b Rhoda Sidney/Stock Boston; 102-103: bkgrd Pascal Quittemelle/Stock Boston; 103: t. B. Christensen/Stock Boston; 104: m. Bob Daemmrich/Stock Boston; 105: b. David Young-Wolff/Photo Edit; 106: r. U.S. Library of Congress; 107: ml. John Elk III/Stock Boston; r. Corbis; 110: br. E. R. Degginger/Dembinsky Photo Associates; bl. JC Carton/Bruce Coleman, Inc.; 110-111: bkgrd Thomas Fletcher/Stock Boston; 111: b. Tom Boyden/Dembinsky Photo Associates; 112: br. David Nunuk/Photo Researchers, Inc.; 120-121: bkgrd Getty Images; 128: b. Lawrence Migdale for MMH; 128-129: t. The Henry E. Huntington Library & Art Gallery; 129: m. Lawrence Migdale for MMH; 134: tr. Richard Cummins/Corbis; 136: bl. Barney Burstein/Corbis; 140: bl. Susan Talbert; br. Susan Talbert; 141: l. Susan Talbert; r. Susan Talbert; 143: tr. Culver Pictures; b. Hulton Archive/Getty Images; 144-145: bkgrd The Granger Collection; 145: tr. Francis G. Mayor/Corbis; 146: b. Superstock; 146-147: bkgrd Joseph Sohm/Corbis; 147: r. Tony Freeman/Photo Edit; 148: b. Getty Images; 150-151: bkgrd PhotoDisc; 151: r. Corbis/Bettman; 152: r. Corbis; 153: t. Art Resource; br. Culver Pictures; 154: l. Philip Gould/Corbis; br. Culver Pictures; 155: r. Philip Gould/Corbis; 156: mr. AP/Wide World Photos; b. Historical Society of Battle Creek; tl. Historical Society of Battle Creek; 157: r. Getty Images; 158-159: bkgrd Getty Images; 160-161: t. Jose Carrillo/Photo Edit; b. Bob Daemmrich/Stock Boston; bl. Nik Wheeler/Corbis; 161: r. Emile Wamsteker/AP/Wide World Photos; 162: r. The Granger Collection; 163: l. Art Resources; br. Corbis; 164-165: bkgrd Ohio Historical Society; 166-167: b. Dawson Jones/Stock Boston; 167: tr. The Granger Collection; 168: bl. Paul Souders/Corbis; l. Bill Bachman/Photo Researchers, Inc.; 169: br. Ralph A. Clevenger/Corbis; tr. Rick Smolan/Stock Boston; ml. Brian Brake/Photo Researchers, Inc.; 170: Joseph Sohm/Corbis; 171: tr. Hulton Archive; 178-179: bkgrd Richard Pasley/Stock Boston; 181: r. Bob Daemmrich; tl. Kathy McLaughlin/Image Works; 184: bl. Amy Etra/Photo Edit; 184-185: t. Hisham F Ibrahim/PhotoDisc; bkgrd Brian Atkinson/Alamay Images; m.r. Bob Daemmrich; 188: bl. David Ulmer/Stock Boston; br. Bob Daemmrich; 189: br. Chris Brown/Stock Boston; m. R. Crandall/Image Works; 190: t.l. Martin Rogers/Stock Boston; t.r. Lawrence Migdale; 191: t.r. Stephen Frisch/Stock Boston; tl. Superstock; 192: Barbara Palmer; 193: ml. Barbara Palmer; 194: b. Steve McAlister/Getty; br. Michael Newman/Photo Edit; 195: m. PhotoDisc; 196: bkgrd Stacy Pick/Stock Boston; 197: ml. Jeff Greenberg/Photo Edit; mr. Jeff Greenberg/Stock Boston; b. Esbin Anderson/Image Works; 202: m. Dick Thomas/Visuals Unlimited, Inc.; mr. Kevin Morris/Corbis; 204-205: b. John Elk III/Stock Boston; 208: bl. Mark E Gibson/Dembinsky Photo Associates; 208-209: m. F. Pedrick/Image Works; 209: r. Greig Cranna/Stock Boston; 210: b. Tom Hollyman/Photo Researchers, Inc.; t. Tommaso Guicciardini/Photo Researchers, Inc.; 210-211: bkgrd Tommaso Guicciardini/Photo Researchers, Inc.; 211: t. Geoff Tompkinson/Photo Researchers, Inc.; 214: br. Bill Gillette/Stock Boston; 214-215: b.l. PhotoDisc; 220: bl. Corbis; bm. FPG International; 220-221: b.m. Corbis; 221: ml. Superstock; bm. Superstock; mr. Tony Freeman/Photo Edit; br. Sonda Dawes/Image Works; 222: br. Getty; t. Tom Tschida/Getty; 223: r. Mike Provost for MMH; 224: tl. Superstock; 224-225: bkgrd Archive Photos; 226: r. Dwight R Cendrowski/Mira; 226-227: bkgrd Keren Su/China Span; 227: m Superstock; 236-237: bkgrd The Granger Collection; 238: m. Uniphoto; 239: m. Newsmakers /Getty Images; 242: mr. courtesy office of Governor Minner; l. Ron Edmonds/AP/Wide World Photos; ml. Paul Grebliunas/Tony Stone Images; r. Robert J. Bennett; 243: br. Corbis; br. Xue Tiejun/PictureQuest; 244: t. Joseph Sohm/Corbis; 245: b. Corbis; t. Corbis/Bettman; 248: bl. Marion Wolcott/Corbis; t. The Granger Collection; 248 -249: b.l. PhotoDisc; 249: m. Supreme Court of the United States; 261: r. R. Morley/PhotoDisc; 262: br. Courtesy of White House Historical Association; bl. Courtesy of White House Historical Association; 263: t. Courtesy of White House Historical Association; b. Courtesy of White House Historical Association; 266-267: bkgrd The Granger Collection; 268: br. Larime Photo/Dembinsky Photo Associates; tr. Bob Elsdale/Image Bank; l. Dallas & John Heaton/Stock Boston; 272: m. PhotoSpin; 273: r. Russ Wilson/Superstock; 274-275: bkgd Francis G. Mayer/Corbis; 275: t Courtesy CBS, Inc.; 276: t. Archive Photos; bkgrd AP/Wide World Photos; r. Erwin C "Bud" Nielsen/Mira; 277: br. Getty Images; 278: b. Corbis/Bettman; 279: t. Philip Jon Bailey/Stock Boston; b. Dave Hammond/AP/Wide World Photos; 280: br. Bettman/ Corbis; bl. AFP/ Corbis; 281: bkgrd Corbis SABA; tl. Richard T. Nowitz/Corbis; ml. Corbis; 282: br. Bob Edme/AP/Wide World Photos; bl. Patrick Gardin/AP/Wide World Photos; br. Bob Edme/AP/Wide World Photos; b/bkgrd Reuters/ HO/Hulton Archive; 284: br. R.Morley/PhotoDisc; 289: t. Peter Vandermark/PictureQuest; 290: Barney Burnstein/Corbis/Burnstein Collection; tl. Kelly Mooney/Corbis; 291: tr. Filip Schulke/Corbis; 292: inset, r. Francis G Mayer/Corbis; tl. Corbis; ml. Dennis Black/PictureQuest; 293: tl. Lawrence Migdale/Mira; 294: t. Mark Wilson/Getty Images; 295: tl. Joe Chromo Sohn/PictureQuest. **Section R:** R10 m. Myrleen Ferguson/Photo Edit; m. The Granger Collection; R11: t. Adam Smith/FPG International; t. Billy Barnes/Stock Boston; R12: m. NASA; m. Edward L Miller/Stock Boston; b. David Nunuk/Photo Researchers, Inc.; b. Stacy Pick/Stock Boston; R13: t. courtesy office of Governor Minner; m. John Elk III/Stock Boston; m. Getty Images; b. Nik Wheeler/Corbis; b. The Granger Collection; R14: t. Chuck Pefley/Stock Boston; t. C. C. Lockwood/Bruce Coleman, Inc.; m. Stephen Graham/Dembinsky Photo Associates; b. PhotoDisc; R15: t. Ron Edmonds/AP/Wide World Photos; t. Joseph Sohm/Stock Boston; m. Walter Bibikow/Stock Boston; b. University Productions; b. Carr Clifton/Minden Pictures; R16: t. Steve McAlister/Getty; m. John Elk III/Stock Boston; m. Barrie Rokeach; b. Getty Images; b. John Elk III/Bruce Coleman, Inc.; b. Culver Pictures; R17: t. David Young-Wolff/Photo Edit; m. John Elk III/Stock Boston; m. Stephen Knox/The Knox Files; m. Jan Halaska/Photo Researchers, Inc.; b. Esbin Anderson/Image Works; b. Rhoda Sidney/Stock Boston; R18: t. Art Resource; m. Stephen Knox/The Knox Files, m. Dallas & John Heaton/Stock Boston; b. Mark Richards/Photo Edit; R19: t. Kelly Mooney/Corbis; t. Superstock; m. Richard Nowitz/National Geographic; m. David Simson/PictureQuest; m. Bob Daemmrich Photo, Inc;. b. PhotoDisc; b. Xue Tiejun/PictureQuest.

Acknowledgments *(continued from page ii)*

From "JCWP Volunteers: Jimmy and Rosalynn Carter." **Jimmy Carter Work Project 1999**. Copyright ©2000 Habitat for Humanity International. June 22, 2001. *www.habitat.org/jcwp/98/friv.html* Used by permission. "Farmworkers" from **Gathering the Sun** by Alma Flor Ada. Copyright ©1997 by Alma Flor Ada. Lothrop, Lee & Shephard Books, a division of William Morrow & Company, Inc. All rights reserved. From "The Status of Women, Past, Present, and Future," The Arena, May 1897. From "Chief Joseph: The Biography of a Great Indian," by Chester Anders Fee. Wilson Erickson 1936. From "I've Been to the Mountaintop" from **A Call to Conscience: The Landmark Speeches of Dr. Martin Luther King, Jr.**, Clayborne Carson and Kris Shepard, eds. IPM/Warner Books, 2001. Copyright © The Estate of Martin Luther King, Jr. Used by permission.